THE SMART MONEY

T.C. Catz
The Smart Money

Published by Spines
ISBN: 979-8-89569-730-6

The Smart Money

AI and Personal Investing: Unlocking the Power of Artificial Intelligence for Better Financial Decisions

T.C. Catz

Contents

Dedication

To those who dare to embrace the future of finance, those who seek knowledge and empower themselves with technology. May this book serve as a guide on your path to financial freedom and success in the age of artificial intelligence.

PREFACE

In an era defined by rapid technological advancements, the financial landscape is undergoing a profound transformation. Artificial intelligence (AI) is no longer a futuristic concept; it is a powerful force reshaping the way we invest, manage our finances, and plan for the future. This book aims to demystify the world of AI in finance and empower individuals to harness its potential for personal wealth creation.

We stand at a pivotal juncture where the intersection of technology and finance holds immense promise. AI offers unparalleled opportunities to streamline investment processes, enhance decision-making, and democratize access to financial services. However, navigating this uncharted territory requires a clear understanding of the tools, strategies, and ethical considerations involved.

This book serves as a comprehensive guide, providing both theoretical knowledge and practical insights into the world of AI-driven personal finance. It is designed for individuals of all financial backgrounds, from beginners seeking to enter the investment world to seasoned investors looking to refine their approach.

We invite you to embark on this journey of discovery, where you will explore the latest advancements in AI-powered financial technologies, learn how to leverage these tools effectively, and gain the knowledge and confidence to make informed investment decisions that align with your financial goals.

Introduction

The financial world is changing, and at the heart of this transformation is artificial intelligence (AI). Once confined to science fiction, AI is now a powerful force reshaping the way we invest, manage our finances, and plan for the future. This book delves into the transformative power of AI in personal finance, providing a comprehensive guide for navigating the complexities of modern investment strategies.

From understanding the basics of personal investing to leveraging AI-powered tools for informed decision-making, this book equips readers with the knowledge and skills needed to confidently navigate the financial landscape. We will explore various investment options, including stocks, bonds, real estate, and mutual funds, and discover how AI algorithms can enhance risk assessment, portfolio optimization, and asset allocation.

This book is not just about AI; it is about empowering individuals to take control of their financial well-being. We will delve into the latest advancements in AI-driven financial technologies, such as robo-advisors, automated trading platforms, and personalized financial recommendations. We will also explore the ethical considerations and potential risks associated with AI in finance, emphasizing the importance of human oversight and financial literacy in the age of AI.

This book is a journey into the future of finance, where AI is not a threat but an opportunity. It is a call to action for individuals to embrace the transformative power of technology and shape their own financial destiny. Through practical insights, real-world examples, and a clear, concise writing style, we aim to equip readers with the knowledge and confidence to harness the power of AI and make informed investment decisions that align with their financial goals.

Why The N.E.R.D.Y. Way?

The **N.E.R.D.Y.** Way, a potent acronym that stands for k**N**owledge, **E**ducation, **R**esource, **D**iscovery for **Y**ou, embodies the spirit of this book. It's not just a journey through the world of AI; it's an invitation to embark on a lifelong adventure of learning, exploration, and constant evolution. As the field of AI progresses at an astonishing pace, so too must our understanding and engagement with it. The NERDY Way encourages you to embrace this dynamic and ever-changing landscape as a catalyst for personal growth and societal advancement.

Think of it as an ongoing dialogue, a conversation between you and the world of AI, where curiosity is your compass and exploration is your guide. This journey is not about reaching a destination; it's about the continuous process of learning, adapting, and evolving alongside the ever-expanding frontiers of AI. Embrace the challenges and opportunities that come with this journey, for within them lies the potential to unlock your own capabilities and contribute to a future where technology empowers humanity.

The N.E.R.D.Y. Way is a mindset, a philosophy that encourages you to approach AI with a sense of wonder and a spirit of inquiry. It's about recognizing the profound impact AI is having on every aspect of our lives and acknowledging its potential to reshape our world. This mindset fosters a deep appreciation for the transformative power of AI while also recognizing the critical need for responsible development and deployment. It's about understanding the intricate workings of AI systems, their strengths, and limitations, and using this knowledge to make informed decisions about their use.

The N.E.R.D.Y. Way isn't just about acquiring knowledge; it's about applying it to create a better future. This journey is about using your understanding of AI to solve global challenges, foster collaboration between humans and machines, and shape a future where technology serves as a force for good. It's about embracing the responsibility that comes with this knowledge, recognizing that AI's future depends on our collective efforts.

For those who choose to embark on this journey, the rewards are boundless. You will gain a deeper understanding of the world around you, develop valuable skills, and contribute to a future where technology serves as a force for good. It's an invitation to join the conversation, to contribute to the dialogue, and to shape the future of AI for the benefit of all. The N.E.R.D.Y. Way is a testament to the power of learning, collaboration, and continuous exploration, a journey that will enrich your life and help build a better future for everyone.

The N.E.R.D.Y. Way isn't just about understanding AI; it's about becoming a part of its evolution, a contributor to its progress, and a champion for its responsible development and deployment. It's a reminder that the future of AI is not a distant prospect; it's happening now, and it's up to us to shape it. It's a call to action, a reminder that we all have a role to play in this journey, and every step we take, every question we ask, every idea we share, helps us move closer to a brighter future.

Chapter 1

Introduction to AI in Personal Finance

The financial landscape is undergoing a dramatic transformation, powered by the relentless rise of artificial intelligence (AI). AI is no longer a futuristic concept; it's weaving itself into the fabric of finance, reshaping how we invest, manage our money, and plan for the future. This technological revolution promises to democratize access to financial services, empowering individuals to take control of their financial well-being like never before.

At the heart of this revolution lies the ability of AI to analyze vast amounts of data at lightning speed, uncovering hidden patterns and insights that would be impossible for humans to discern. AI algorithms can sift through mountains of financial data, market trends, economic indicators, and individual financial profiles, identifying opportunities and risks with unparalleled accuracy. This data-driven approach allows for more informed investment decisions, customized financial recommendations, and a level of personalization that was unimaginable just a few years ago.

Imagine a world where your financial decisions are no longer driven by emotions or gut feelings but by objective, data-driven analysis. This is the promise of AI in finance. Imagine AI algorithms analyzing your financial history, risk tolerance, and investment goals to create a personalized investment portfolio that aligns perfectly with your needs. This personalized approach goes beyond traditional financial advice, providing a tailored roadmap to financial success.

AI is revolutionizing personal investing in several key ways:

- **Robo-advisors:** These AI-powered platforms offer automated financial advice and portfolio management services at a fraction of the cost of traditional advisors. By leveraging algorithms, robo-advisors can analyze your financial situation, set investment goals, and create a diversified portfolio tailored to your risk tolerance. They continuously monitor and adjust your portfolio based on market conditions and your evolving needs, ensuring your investments remain aligned with your objectives.
- **Automated trading platforms:** These platforms utilize AI algorithms to execute trades automatically based on predefined strategies. This allows investors to leverage the power of AI to capitalize on market opportunities, even when they are not actively monitoring their portfolios. The algorithms can analyze vast amounts of data in real-time, identifying profitable trading opportunities and executing trades with precision and speed.
- **AI-driven market analysis:** AI algorithms can analyze market trends, identify investment

opportunities, and predict market movements with remarkable accuracy. They can scour news articles, financial reports, social media feeds, and economic data to identify patterns and signals that might be missed by human analysts. This data-driven approach allows investors to make informed decisions, capitalizing on emerging trends and avoiding potential pitfalls.

The benefits of AI in finance are undeniable, but it's crucial to acknowledge the potential challenges and ethical considerations that accompany this technological advancement.

One of the primary concerns is the risk of bias in AI algorithms. These algorithms are trained on vast datasets, and if these datasets contain biases, those biases can be reflected in the algorithms' outputs. For example, an algorithm trained on historical data that reflects gender-based discrimination in the financial sector could perpetuate those biases in its recommendations.

Another concern is the potential for AI-driven financial systems to be vulnerable to cyberattacks and data breaches. The reliance on vast amounts of data makes these systems attractive targets for malicious actors, highlighting the importance of robust cybersecurity measures to protect sensitive financial information.

Furthermore, there are ethical considerations surrounding the use of AI in financial decision-making. As AI algorithms become more sophisticated, the question arises: how much control should we relinquish to these algorithms? What happens when AI makes decisions that are unexpected or counterintuitive? This raises questions about accountability, transparency, and the need for human oversight in the decision-making process.

Despite these challenges, the potential benefits of AI in finance are immense. AI has the power to democratize access to financial services, empowering individuals to take control of their finances, regardless of their income level or financial literacy. AI-powered tools can provide personalized financial advice, automated portfolio management, and data-driven insights that were previously available only to wealthy individuals with access to sophisticated financial advisors.

The future of finance is intertwined with AI. By embracing this technology, individuals can unlock new opportunities for financial success, navigating the complexities of the financial world with greater confidence and control. This book serves as your guide to understanding the transformative power of AI in personal finance, empowering you to make informed decisions and build a secure financial future.

The Rise of AI in Finance

The financial industry is on the cusp of a technological revolution, driven by the relentless advance of artificial intelligence (AI). AI is no longer a futuristic concept; it's weaving itself into the fabric of finance, reshaping how we invest, manage our money, and plan for the future. This transformation is driven by the ability of AI to analyze vast amounts of data at lightning speed, uncovering hidden patterns and insights that would be impossible for humans to discern.

Imagine a world where your financial decisions are no longer driven by emotions or gut feelings but by objective, data-driven analysis. This is the promise of AI in finance. Imagine AI algorithms analyzing your financial history, risk tolerance, and investment goals to create a personalized investment portfolio that aligns perfectly with your needs. This personalized approach goes beyond traditional financial advice, providing a tailored roadmap to financial success.

The Evolution of AI in Finance:

AI's journey in finance began with rudimentary systems designed to automate simple tasks, such as data entry and trade execution. However, the rapid advancements in machine learning and deep learning have propelled AI to new heights, enabling it to tackle more complex financial challenges.

Here are some key milestones in the evolution of AI in finance:

- **Early Days (1980s-1990s):** The early days of AI in finance were characterized by rule-based systems designed to automate specific tasks, such as trade execution and fraud detection. These systems were limited in their ability to adapt to changing market conditions and learn from new data.
- **The Rise of Machine Learning (2000s):** The advent of machine learning algorithms brought a new level of sophistication to AI in finance. These algorithms could learn from historical data, identify patterns, and make predictions. This led to the development of tools like credit scoring models, risk management systems, and automated trading strategies.
- **Deep Learning and Big Data (2010s-Present):** The rise of deep learning algorithms and the availability of massive datasets have further revolutionized AI in finance. These algorithms can analyze complex data patterns, identify subtle relationships, and make more accurate predictions. This has enabled the

development of sophisticated tools for fraud detection, portfolio optimization, and personalized financial recommendations.

The Impact of AI on Financial Institutions

AI is transforming financial institutions of all sizes, from large banks and investment firms to smaller fintech startups. These institutions are leveraging AI to:

- **Improve efficiency and reduce costs:** AI can automate tasks like data entry, customer service, and trade execution, freeing up human employees to focus on more complex and strategic activities.
- **Enhance risk management:** AI algorithms can analyze vast amounts of data to identify potential risks and vulnerabilities, allowing financial institutions to take proactive measures to mitigate these risks.
- **Personalize customer experiences:** AI-powered chatbots and virtual assistants can provide personalized customer service, offering tailored financial advice and recommendations.
- **Develop new products and services:** AI is enabling financial institutions to create innovative products and services, such as AI-driven robo-advisors and personalized investment platforms.

The Benefits of AI in Finance

The benefits of AI in finance are far-reaching, impacting both financial institutions and individual investors. These benefits include:

- **Increased efficiency and productivity:** AI can automate tasks, reduce errors, and free up human employees to focus on more strategic activities.
- **Improved decision-making:** AI algorithms can analyze vast amounts of data to identify opportunities and risks, providing more accurate and informed decision-making.
- **Enhanced risk management:** AI can help financial institutions identify and mitigate potential risks, protecting their assets and reputation.
- **Democratized access to financial services:** AI-powered tools can provide personalized financial advice and services at a fraction of the cost of traditional advisors, making these services accessible to a wider range of individuals.
- **Increased transparency and accountability:** AI-driven systems can provide transparent and auditable records of financial decisions, increasing accountability and reducing the potential for fraud.

The Challenges of AI in Finance

While the benefits of AI in finance are undeniable, there are also significant challenges that need to be addressed:

- **Bias in AI algorithms:** AI algorithms are trained on vast datasets, and if these datasets contain biases, those biases can be reflected in the algorithms' outputs. For example, an algorithm trained on historical data that reflects gender-based discrimination in the financial sector could perpetuate those biases in its recommendations.

- **Cybersecurity risks:** The reliance on vast amounts of data makes AI-driven financial systems attractive targets for malicious actors. Robust cybersecurity measures are crucial to protect sensitive financial information.
- **Ethical considerations:** As AI algorithms become more sophisticated, the question arises: how much control should we relinquish to these algorithms? What happens when AI makes decisions that are unexpected or counterintuitive? This raises questions about accountability, transparency, and the need for human oversight in the decision-making process.

The future of finance is intertwined with AI. By embracing this technology, individuals can unlock new opportunities for financial success, navigating the complexities of the financial world with greater confidence and control. This book serves as your guide to understanding the transformative power of AI in personal finance, empowering you to make informed decisions and build a secure financial future.

AI and Personal Investing

Imagine a world where your financial decisions are powered by the same advanced technology that drives self-driving cars and personalized recommendations on your favorite streaming platforms. This is the reality taking shape in the world of personal finance, thanks to the rise of Artificial Intelligence (AI). AI is no longer just a futuristic concept; it's a tangible force reshaping how we manage our money, invest for the future, and navigate the complexities of the financial landscape.

AI's foray into personal investing is a transformative partnership, ushering in an era where algorithms can analyze vast amounts of data, identify investment opportunities, and personalize financial strategies like never before. Gone are the days of sifting through reams of financial reports or relying solely on gut feelings. AI-powered tools are revolutionizing the investment process, empowering individuals with data-driven insights and automated solutions.

At the heart of this transformation lies the power of data analysis. AI algorithms can process information from countless sources – market trends, economic indicators, company performance, and even social media sentiment – to uncover hidden patterns and predict future market movements. This ability to analyze vast quantities of data far surpasses human capacity, offering investors a distinct edge.

One of the most prominent applications of AI in personal investing is the emergence of robo-advisors. These automated platforms leverage sophisticated algorithms to create personalized investment portfolios tailored to individual risk tolerance and investment goals. They eliminate the need for expensive financial advisors, making professional investment management accessible to a broader audience.

Robo-advisors operate on a set of predefined rules and algorithms, constantly analyzing market conditions and rebalancing portfolios to maintain optimal asset allocation. Their automated nature ensures consistent and objective decision-making, free from human biases and emotional influences that can cloud judgment.

Beyond robo-advisors, AI is transforming various aspects of the investment process, from automated trading to personalized financial recommendations. AI-driven trading platforms can execute trades with lightning speed based on predefined strategies, maximizing efficiency and minimizing human error. These platforms leverage real-time market data, analyze historical trends, and identify profitable trading opportunities, often surpassing the performance of human traders.

Personalization is another key aspect of AI's impact on investing. AI algorithms can analyze individual financial profiles, investment goals, and risk tolerance to deliver customized recommendations and financial advice. This level of personalization ensures that investment strategies are tailored to specific needs, maximizing the likelihood of achieving desired outcomes.

AI-powered tools can analyze personal financial data, including income, expenses, and existing investments, to identify areas for improvement. They can provide tailored recommendations for budgeting, saving, and debt management, helping individuals optimize their financial health.

However, the integration of AI in personal investing is not without its challenges and ethical considerations. While AI offers immense potential, it's crucial to acknowledge the potential risks associated with relying solely on algorithms for financial decisions.

One key concern is the possibility of bias in AI algorithms. If the data used to train these algorithms is biased, the resulting recommendations may be skewed, potentially leading to unfavorable outcomes for investors. It's crucial to ensure that AI algorithms are developed and trained using diverse and representative data to minimize the risk of bias.

Another concern is the lack of transparency in AI decision-making. Many AI algorithms operate as "black boxes," making it difficult to understand how they arrive at their conclusions. This lack of transparency raises questions about accountability and the potential for unintended consequences.

Moreover, the rapid evolution of AI technologies demands continuous learning and adaptation. Investors need to stay informed about the latest advancements and understand how these technologies can be applied to their investment strategies. Financial literacy plays a critical role in navigating the complexities of AI-driven finance, ensuring informed decision-making and responsible use of these powerful tools.

Despite these challenges, the transformative potential of AI in personal investing is undeniable. AI algorithms are revolutionizing the way we analyze market data, identify opportunities, and manage our investments. With the right understanding and approach, AI can become a powerful ally in our financial journey, helping us navigate the complexities of the market, make informed decisions, and achieve our financial goals.

The future of personal investing lies in harnessing the power of AI while maintaining a balanced approach. While AI algorithms can provide valuable insights and automate certain tasks, human judgment, financial literacy, and a deep understanding of personal circumstances remain crucial for successful investment decision-making. Embracing this partnership between human expertise and AI technology can pave the way for a brighter financial future, empowered by data, innovation, and a personalized approach to investment success.

Understanding the Fundamentals of Personal Finance

Understanding the fundamentals of personal finance is the cornerstone of achieving financial well-being. It lays the foundation for informed decision-making, responsible money management, and ultimately, achieving your financial goals. This section delves into the core principles of personal finance, providing a comprehensive understanding of budgeting, saving, and debt management.

The Art of Budgeting

Budgeting is the process of creating a plan for your income and expenses, ensuring that you spend less than you earn. A well-structured budget acts as a roadmap for your financial life, helping you prioritize spending, track your progress, and stay in control of your finances. Here's how budgeting works:

1. **Track your income:** The first step involves identifying all sources of income, whether it's your salary, investments, or any other form of income.
2. **Categorize your expenses:** Next, categorize your expenses, differentiating between fixed expenses, such as rent or mortgage payments, and variable expenses, such as groceries or entertainment.
3. **Create a spending plan:** Allocate your income to each category based on your priorities and needs. This process involves making deliberate choices about how you allocate your money.
4. **Monitor and adjust:** Regularly monitor your spending against your budget and make adjustments as

needed. This ensures that your budget remains relevant and reflects your changing circumstances.

The Power of Saving

Saving money is the key to achieving your financial goals, be it buying a house, funding your retirement, or pursuing your dreams. Savings provide a financial safety net, ensuring you have the resources to weather unforeseen circumstances and achieve your long-term aspirations. Here's a breakdown of the principles of saving:

1. **Set realistic savings goals:** Start by defining your financial goals. Are you saving for a down payment on a house, a comfortable retirement, or a dream vacation? Having specific goals will motivate you and give your saving efforts a clear direction.

2. **Automate your savings:** Setting up automatic transfers from your checking account to your savings account is a powerful way to ensure consistent saving. By automating the process, you'll avoid the temptation to spend the money before it reaches your savings.

3. **Explore different savings vehicles:** Consider various savings vehicles, such as high-yield savings accounts, certificates of deposit (CDs), and money market accounts. Each option offers varying interest rates and terms, allowing you to choose the best fit for your financial needs.

4. **Make savings a habit:** Consistency is key to building wealth. Treat saving as a non-negotiable part of your monthly budget, just like paying your rent or mortgage.

Managing Debt Effectively

Debt can be a powerful tool, but it can also become a heavy burden if not managed responsibly. Learning to manage debt effectively is crucial for maintaining financial stability and achieving long-term financial goals. Here's a guide to responsible debt management:

1. **Understand the types of debt:** Different types of debt carry different interest rates and terms. Differentiate between good debt, such as a mortgage or student loan, and bad debt, such as credit card debt.
2. **Prioritize debt repayment:** Focus on paying down high-interest debt first, as it accumulates interest more quickly. Employ strategies like debt consolidation or snowballing to reduce the interest burden.
3. **Avoid unnecessary debt:** Resist the temptation to accumulate unnecessary debt through impulsive purchases or frivolous spending. Be conscious of your spending habits and avoid falling into the trap of overspending.
4. **Develop a debt repayment plan:** Creating a realistic repayment plan, with specific milestones and deadlines, can help you stay on track and motivated.

Harnessing the Power of Compound Interest

Compound interest is often referred to as the "eighth wonder of the world," and for good reason. It's the ability of interest earned on an investment to generate further interest over time. This exponential growth can work wonders in accumulating wealth, but it requires patience, discipline, and a long-term perspective.

1. **Time is your ally:** The longer your money is invested, the more time it has to compound, leading to significant growth over the years.
2. **Even small amounts matter:** Don't underestimate the power of consistent savings, even if they're small. Every dollar invested has the potential to grow exponentially through compounding.
3. **Seek out higher returns:** While prioritizing safety, aim to invest your money in assets that offer a reasonable return, enabling faster compounding and accelerating wealth growth.

The Importance of Financial Literacy

In an increasingly complex financial landscape, financial literacy is more important than ever. It's the ability to understand financial concepts, make informed decisions, and manage your money effectively. Here's why financial literacy is critical:

1. **Empowering yourself with knowledge:** Financial literacy equips you with the tools and knowledge to make informed financial decisions, allowing you to take control of your financial well-being.
2. **Avoiding costly mistakes:** A lack of financial literacy can lead to poor financial decisions, resulting in unnecessary debt, missed investment opportunities, and ultimately, financial hardship.
3. **Achieving long-term financial goals:** Financial literacy empowers you to set realistic financial goals, develop a strategy to achieve them, and track your progress along the way.

Integrating AI into your Personal Finance: While the fundamentals of personal finance remain essential, AI technology is revolutionizing how we manage our finances. AI-powered tools can automate tasks, analyze data, and provide personalized insights, making it easier to manage your money effectively and achieve your financial goals.

1. **Harnessing AI's potential:** Automated budgeting and expense tracking: AI-driven apps can categorize your spending, track your income and expenses, and provide insights into your financial behavior.
2. **Personalized financial advice:** Robo-advisors utilize AI algorithms to create personalized investment portfolios based on your risk tolerance, time horizon, and financial goals.
3. **Market analysis and investment insights:** AI-powered platforms can analyze market trends, identify investment opportunities, and generate personalized financial recommendations.
4. **The future of personal finance:** The integration of AI is transforming personal finance, making it more accessible, efficient, and data-driven. By embracing AI, we can streamline our financial management, gain valuable insights, and take control of our financial future.

Conclusion

Understanding the fundamentals of personal finance is crucial for achieving financial well-being. By embracing budgeting, saving, and debt management, we lay the foundation for a secure financial future. AI technology is further revolutionizing how we manage our money, offering powerful tools for automating tasks, gaining insights, and making informed financial decisions. As we move forward into an era of AI-driven finance, it's essential to remain informed and adaptable, harnessing the power of both traditional and emerging technologies to create a brighter financial future.

INVESTMENT BASICS

Investing is the act of committing money or resources to an asset with the expectation of generating future income or appreciation in value. It's a crucial aspect of personal finance, as it allows individuals to grow their wealth over time and achieve their financial goals. However, the world of investing can seem daunting, especially for beginners. This section provides a comprehensive overview of the fundamental investment options, serving as a starting point for your investment journey.

Stocks: Stocks represent ownership in a publicly traded company. When you purchase a stock, you become a shareholder, entitled to a portion of the company's profits and assets. Stocks are known for their potential for high returns, but they also carry higher risk compared to other investment options.

Types of Stocks

- **Common Stock:** The most common type of stock, offering voting rights in company decisions and a share of profits through dividends.
- **Preferred Stock:** A type of stock that pays a fixed dividend, offering a more stable income stream but usually with limited voting rights.

Investing in Stocks

- **Direct Investing:** Purchasing stocks directly through a brokerage account, allowing you to choose individual companies.
- **Mutual Funds:** Investing in a diversified portfolio of stocks managed by a professional fund manager.
- **Exchange-Traded Funds (ETFs):** Similar to mutual funds, but traded on stock exchanges like individual stocks.

Bonds: Bonds are debt securities issued by governments, corporations, or other entities to raise capital. When you purchase a bond, you essentially lend money to the issuer and receive regular interest payments in return. Bonds are generally considered less risky than stocks, offering a more stable income stream.

Types of Bonds

- **Government Bonds:** Issued by federal, state, or local governments, considered relatively safe investments.
- **Corporate Bonds:** Issued by corporations to finance operations, carrying a higher risk than government bonds but potentially offering higher returns.

Investing in Bonds

- **Individual Bonds:** Buying individual bonds directly through a brokerage account.
- **Bond Funds:** Investing in a diversified portfolio of bonds managed by a professional fund manager.

Real Estate: Real estate investment involves purchasing properties such as houses, apartments, or commercial buildings with the expectation of generating rental income, appreciation in value, or both. Real estate can provide a tangible asset with the potential for long-term growth, but it also requires significant capital investment and ongoing management.

Types of Real Estate Investments

- **Residential Real Estate:** Investing in properties for residential use, such as single-family homes or apartment buildings.
- **Commercial Real Estate:** Investing in properties used for business purposes, such as office buildings, retail stores, or industrial warehouses.
- **Real Estate Investment Trusts (REITs):** Companies that own and operate income-producing real estate, providing investors with exposure to the real estate market through publicly traded shares.

Investing in Real Estate

- **Direct Ownership:** Purchasing a property outright or taking out a mortgage to finance it.
- **Real Estate Crowdfunding:** Investing in real estate projects through online platforms, allowing for smaller investments in diversified portfolios.
- **Understanding Risk and Return:** Investment decisions involve balancing risk and return. High-risk investments, such as stocks, have the potential for high returns, but they also carry a higher chance of losing

money. Low-risk investments, such as bonds, generally offer lower returns but provide greater stability.

- **Diversification:** Diversification is a key principle in investing, involving spreading your investments across different asset classes (stocks, bonds, real estate) and sectors (industries) to reduce overall risk. By diversifying your portfolio, you reduce the impact of any single investment on your overall returns.

- **Time Horizon:** Your investment time horizon is the length of time you plan to hold your investments. Your time horizon plays a significant role in determining your investment strategy. Long-term investors (those with a time horizon of 5-10 years or more) can generally afford to take on more risk, while short-term investors (those with a time horizon of less than 5 years) typically prefer lower-risk investments.

- **Market Research:** Before making any investment decisions, it's essential to conduct thorough market research. This involves staying informed about current economic conditions, industry trends, and the performance of specific companies or assets. Market research helps you identify potential investment opportunities and assess the risks involved.

- **Professional Advice:** While this section provides a starting point for your investment journey, seeking professional advice from a certified financial advisor is always recommended, especially for those new to investing. A financial advisor can help you develop a personalized investment strategy that aligns with your financial goals, risk tolerance, and time horizon.

CONCLUSION

This section provided a foundational understanding of the key investment options available, equipping you with the knowledge to embark on your investment journey. Remember, investing is a long-term process that requires patience, discipline, and a thoughtful approach. By understanding the different investment options, assessing risk, and seeking professional advice, you can create a diversified portfolio that aligns with your financial goals and helps you build wealth over time.

SETTING FINANCIAL GOALS

Imagine a world where your financial goals are no longer abstract dreams, but tangible milestones on a clear roadmap. A world where AI, with its lightning-fast processing power and data analysis prowess, acts as your personal financial navigator, guiding you through the complex landscape of investments and helping you chart a course towards financial freedom.

This is the promise of AI in personal finance, a field that's rapidly evolving, offering individuals unprecedented opportunities to take control of their financial futures. But before we dive into the exciting world of AI-powered tools and strategies, we must first lay the groundwork for success. That means understanding the fundamental principles of personal finance and, most importantly, defining your financial goals.

After all, just as a ship without a destination is adrift at sea, an investment strategy without clear objectives is destined to wander aimlessly. Setting financial goals is the first crucial step in your journey toward financial empowerment.

Think of your financial goals as the North Star guiding your financial compass. They provide direction, motivation, and a sense of purpose for your investment decisions. But setting goals is just the beginning. You need to create a comprehensive strategy that outlines the steps you'll take to achieve them.

Here's where the power of AI comes in:

- **Personalization:** AI can help you set tailored financial goals based on your individual circumstances, risk tolerance, and time horizon. Are you saving for a dream home, a comfortable retirement, or perhaps a child's education? AI can analyze your financial profile and suggest personalized goals that align with your aspirations.
- **Data-Driven Insights:** AI's ability to analyze vast amounts of data empowers you to make more informed decisions. Want to see how your current investment choices measure up against historical market trends? AI can provide insightful comparisons, helping you identify potential areas for improvement.
- **Automated Planning:** AI-powered tools can automate the process of creating and adjusting your financial plan as your circumstances change. This includes budgeting, saving, and even investing. Imagine having a virtual financial assistant constantly working behind the scenes, optimizing your investments and adjusting your plan based on real-time market fluctuations.

Let's delve into the process of setting financial goals using a framework that combines the best of human intuition with the power of AI:

1. Define Your "Why":

Begin by asking yourself: What are you ultimately striving for with your finances? What dreams, aspirations, or goals motivate you to invest your time and money?

This is where your "why" comes into play. Are you seeking to achieve financial independence, secure your family's future, or simply create a comfortable retirement lifestyle?

The clearer your "why," the more compelling your financial goals will become, driving you towards action.

2. Categorize Your Goals:

Once you've identified your overarching "why," it's time to break down your financial aspirations into specific, measurable, achievable, relevant, and time-bound (SMART) goals.

This categorization process allows you to focus your efforts on each individual goal, creating actionable plans for each.

3. Set Short-Term and Long-Term Goals:

This process of goal setting shouldn't feel overwhelming. Think about it as a journey. Break down your long-term goals into shorter, more manageable steps. This approach helps you stay motivated and track your progress.

For example, if your long-term goal is to retire comfortably, you might set shorter-term goals such as saving a specific amount each month or increasing your investment portfolio by a certain percentage.

4. Utilize AI Tools for Goal Planning:

This is where AI can truly enhance your goal-setting process. AI-powered financial planning tools can analyze your current financial situation, your risk tolerance, and your time horizon, providing personalized recommendations for achieving your goals.

These tools can also help you track your progress toward your goals, providing regular updates and suggesting adjustments as needed.

5. Review and Adjust:

Remember, your financial goals and strategies are not set in stone. As your life circumstances change, it's essential to revisit your goals and make necessary adjustments.

This ongoing review process ensures that your financial plan remains relevant and aligned with your evolving needs and aspirations. AI can automate much of this review process, alerting you to potential adjustments based on changes in market conditions or your personal financial situation.

Here are some real-world examples to illustrate how you can use AI to achieve your financial goals:

- **Retirement Planning:** Let's say you're aiming to retire comfortably at age 65. AI-powered retirement planning tools can analyze your current savings, projected income, and expected expenses, creating a personalized plan that outlines the steps you need to take to achieve your retirement goals.
- **Debt Reduction:** Do you have student loan debt or credit card debt that you're trying to pay off? AI-

powered debt management tools can create a debt repayment plan, factoring in your interest rates, monthly payments, and income, helping you prioritize debt repayment and accelerate your path to financial freedom.

- **Saving for a Down Payment:** Dream of owning a home? AI-powered savings calculators can help you determine how much you need to save each month to reach your down payment goal within your desired time frame.

Remember, your financial journey is unique to you. Embrace the power of AI as your guide, but don't forget to listen to your own intuition. With clear goals and a well-defined strategy, you'll be well on your way to achieving financial success. AI is a powerful tool, but ultimately, your financial future is in your hands.

CHAPTER 2

AI-POWERED TOOLS FOR INFORMED DECISION MAKING

In the realm of personal finance, where financial decisions are often fraught with uncertainty, robo-advisors have emerged as a beacon of automated guidance. These AI-powered platforms, designed to simplify and streamline the investment process, have become increasingly popular, offering a compelling alternative to traditional financial advisors.

Robo-advisors utilize sophisticated algorithms to analyze vast amounts of data, including market trends, investment performance, and individual risk profiles. They then leverage this information to generate customized investment recommendations and manage portfolios automatically, eliminating the need for human intervention. This automated approach not only saves time and reduces costs but also minimizes the potential for emotional biases that can cloud human decision-making.

THE ADVANTAGES OF ROBO-ADVISORS

Accessibility and Affordability: Robo-advisors break down the traditional barriers to financial advising, making professional investment management accessible to individuals with a wide range of assets. Their low minimum investment requirements and flat-fee structures eliminate the high fees associated with traditional advisors, making them particularly appealing to younger investors and those with modest portfolios.

Diversification and Portfolio Optimization: Robo-advisors excel at building diversified portfolios, carefully allocating investments across different asset classes to mitigate risk and maximize returns. Using AI algorithms, they analyze individual risk tolerance, investment goals, and time horizon to construct portfolios tailored to specific needs.

Automated Rebalancing: Investing involves continuous adjustments to maintain a desired asset allocation. Robo-advisors automate this process, ensuring that portfolios stay balanced and aligned with evolving market conditions. They monitor market fluctuations and automatically rebalance portfolios to reflect changing risk appetites and investment goals.

Risk Management and Monitoring: Robo-advisors employ AI to monitor market conditions and identify potential risks. They use sophisticated algorithms to assess the overall market environment and identify potential threats to portfolio performance, enabling proactive risk management strategies.

Personalized Insights and Recommendations: Robo-advisors provide personalized insights and recommendations based on individual financial data. They analyze spending habits, income streams, and investment goals to offer tailored advice that promotes financial well-being.

Transparency and Accountability: Robo-advisors typically offer transparent reporting, providing clear insights into portfolio performance and investment strategies. This transparency fosters trust and accountability, enabling investors to understand the rationale behind their investment decisions.

The Role of Robo-Advisors in Portfolio Management

Robo-advisors play a crucial role in portfolio management by providing automated solutions to the complexities of investment decision-making. They utilize AI algorithms to analyze market data, identify investment opportunities, and allocate assets strategically. This automated approach streamlines the investment process, reducing the burden on individual investors and promoting efficient portfolio management.

The Evolution of Robo-Advisors: From Automation to Personalized Financial Guidance

The initial generation of robo-advisors focused on automating basic investment processes such as asset allocation and portfolio rebalancing. However, as AI technologies have evolved, robo-advisors have become increasingly sophisticated, incorporating personalized features and advanced capabilities.

Modern robo-advisors go beyond automated portfolio management, offering a range of personalized financial services, including:

- **Personalized Financial Planning:** Robo-advisors can now create personalized financial plans that address individual financial goals, such as retirement planning, college savings, or purchasing a home.
- **Goal-Based Investing:** Robo-advisors can create investment portfolios tailored to specific financial goals, ensuring that investments align with desired outcomes.
- **Financial Education and Support:** Some robo-advisors offer access to educational resources, financial tools, and expert guidance to enhance financial literacy and empower individuals to make informed investment decisions.
- **Hybrid Robo-Advisors:** The line between robo-advisors and traditional financial advisors is blurring as hybrid platforms emerge. These platforms combine the automation and efficiency of robo-advisors with the personalized advice and human touch of traditional financial advisors.

Choosing the Right Robo-Advisor: Key Considerations

With a growing number of robo-advisors vying for investors' attention, choosing the right platform can be a daunting task. Here are some key considerations:

- **Investment Philosophy and Strategies:** Understand the underlying investment philosophy and strategies employed by the robo-advisor. Do they align with your risk tolerance and investment goals?
- **Asset Classes and Investment Options:** Assess the range of asset classes and investment options available

through the platform. Does it offer the flexibility to build a diversified portfolio that meets your needs?

- **Fees and Minimum Investment Requirements:** Compare fees and minimum investment requirements across different platforms to find the most affordable and accessible solution.
- **Customer Support and Resources:** Evaluate the level of customer support and educational resources provided by the robo-advisor. Do they offer easy access to information and assistance when needed?
- **Security and Data Privacy:** Ensure the platform adheres to robust security measures to protect your financial data and personal information.

The Future of Robo-Advisors: AI-Powered Financial Guidance for Everyone

As AI technology continues to advance, robo-advisors are poised to play an increasingly important role in shaping the future of personal finance. They have the potential to democratize access to financial services, empowering individuals of all financial backgrounds to make informed investment decisions and take control of their financial futures.

The future of robo-advisors promises to be filled with innovation, with platforms becoming increasingly personalized, intuitive, and user-friendly. AI-driven technologies will continue to enhance their capabilities, enabling them to offer more comprehensive financial planning, personalized investment recommendations, and sophisticated risk management strategies.

Robo-advisors are a powerful tool for anyone seeking to navigate the complexities of personal investing. By harnessing the power of AI, they can help individuals streamline their investment process, diversify their portfolios, and achieve their financial goals. As technology advances and robo-advisors become increasingly sophisticated, their impact on the world of personal finance is likely to be profound, making financial guidance more accessible, affordable, and effective for everyone.

AUTOMATED TRADING PLATFORMS

Imagine a world where your investments are managed by a tireless, analytical, and perpetually learning machine. This isn't science fiction; it's the reality of automated trading platforms, where AI algorithms execute trades based on predefined strategies and real-time market data. These platforms operate with remarkable speed and efficiency, making decisions that can outpace even the most experienced human trader.

The Rise of Automated Trading: From Algorithms to Artificial Intelligence

Automated trading has been around for decades, initially relying on simple algorithms to execute orders based on pre-programmed rules. Think of these early systems as "if-then" statements, where if a certain condition is met (like the price of a stock reaching a specific threshold), the algorithm automatically triggers a buy or sell order.

But the arrival of AI has revolutionized automated trading, ushering in a new era of sophisticated trading platforms capable of learning and adapting to constantly evolving market conditions. AI algorithms can analyze vast amounts of data, including historical market trends, news sentiment, economic indicators, and even social media chatter, to identify patterns and predict future price movements. This data-driven approach allows AI to make more informed decisions than traditional rule-based algorithms, potentially leading to improved trading performance.

How AI-Powered Trading Platforms Work

At the heart of an AI-powered trading platform lies a complex neural network, a sophisticated mathematical model designed to mimic the workings of the human brain. These networks are trained on massive datasets of historical market data, allowing them to learn the underlying relationships and patterns that influence price movements. Once trained, the AI can analyze real-time market data and make trading decisions based on its understanding of market dynamics.

Here's a simplified breakdown of the process:

- **Data Collection:** The AI platform gathers data from various sources, including stock exchanges, news feeds, social media, and economic reports.
- **Data Preprocessing:** The raw data is cleaned, standardized, and transformed into a format suitable for analysis by the AI algorithm.
- **Pattern Recognition:** The AI algorithm analyzes the preprocessed data, identifying patterns and correlations that may indicate future price movements.
- **Trading Strategy Development:** Based on its analysis, the AI develops a trading strategy, which includes specific rules for entering and exiting trades.
- **Trade Execution:** The AI automatically executes trades based on the pre-defined strategy, taking advantage of market opportunities as they arise.

- **Performance Monitoring:** The AI platform constantly monitors the performance of its trading strategies, making adjustments and improvements based on real-time results.

Advantages of Automated Trading Platforms:

- **Speed and Efficiency:** AI algorithms can execute trades at lightning speed, capitalizing on fleeting market opportunities that may be missed by human traders.
- **Emotional Detachment:** AI algorithms are not susceptible to emotional biases, like fear or greed, that can cloud human judgment and lead to poor trading decisions.
- **Data-Driven Decision-Making:** AI platforms can process massive amounts of data, identifying subtle patterns and correlations that humans may miss, leading to more informed trading decisions.
- **Continuous Learning:** AI algorithms continuously learn and adapt to new market conditions, improving their performance over time.
- **Customization:** Many AI-powered trading platforms offer a high degree of customization, allowing users to define their own risk tolerance, investment goals, and trading strategies.

Types of AI-Powered Trading Platforms

There are various types of automated trading platforms available, each catering to different levels of experience and investment goals. Here are a few examples:

- **Robo-advisors:** These platforms provide automated portfolio management services, often with a low minimum investment requirement. They typically use AI algorithms to create and manage diversified portfolios based on individual risk tolerance and investment goals.
- **Algorithmic Trading Platforms:** These platforms offer advanced tools for developing and executing automated trading strategies, often used by professional traders and hedge funds.
- **AI-Powered Trading Bots:** These are software programs designed to execute trades automatically based on predefined rules or AI algorithms. They can be used for various trading strategies, from simple trend-following to complex arbitrage strategies.

The Ethical Considerations and Risks of Automated Trading

While AI-powered trading platforms offer numerous advantages, it's essential to acknowledge the ethical considerations and potential risks associated with their use.

Algorithmic Bias: AI algorithms are trained on data, and if the data contains biases, these biases can be reflected in the algorithm's decisions. This can lead to unfair or discriminatory trading outcomes.

Privacy Concerns: AI platforms often collect and process large amounts of personal data, raising concerns about privacy and data security.

Black Box Problem: The complex nature of AI algorithms can

make it difficult to understand why a particular decision was made, raising concerns about transparency and accountability.

Market Volatility: The stock market is inherently volatile, and AI algorithms may not always be able to predict future price movements accurately. This can lead to significant losses, especially during periods of high market volatility.

Job Displacement: The increased use of AI in trading may lead to job displacement for human traders, particularly those performing repetitive or data-intensive tasks.

Striking a Balance: Human Expertise and AI Collaboration

Despite these concerns, AI-powered trading platforms offer significant potential for enhancing investment returns. The key is to strike a balance between human expertise and AI capabilities. Human traders can provide context, intuition, and emotional intelligence, while AI can handle the complex calculations and data analysis required for informed trading decisions.

Ultimately, the most effective approach is one that leverages the strengths of both human and AI, allowing investors to make more informed investment decisions and potentially maximize their returns. The future of investment is a collaborative one, where humans and AI work together to navigate the complex and ever-changing world of finance.

AI-Driven Market Analysis

Imagine a world where data speaks volumes about the market's every move. This is the realm of AI-driven market analysis, where sophisticated algorithms sift through vast amounts of data, identifying patterns and trends that human eyes might miss. It's like having a financial detective working tirelessly to uncover hidden insights and potential investment opportunities.

AI algorithms are adept at processing data from multiple sources, including historical market prices, economic indicators, news sentiment, and even social media trends. By analyzing this wealth of information, they can paint a picture of the market's current state and predict potential future movements. This ability to glean insights from seemingly disparate data points is what sets AI apart.

One of the most exciting aspects of AI-driven market analysis is its ability to identify market anomalies. AI algorithms can detect unusual patterns and price fluctuations that might indicate opportunities or risks. For example, an algorithm might flag a sudden surge in trading volume for a particular stock, suggesting a potential shift in investor sentiment. This early warning system can be invaluable for investors, enabling them to capitalize on emerging trends or avoid potential pitfalls.

Furthermore, AI can analyze historical market data to identify recurring patterns and seasonalities. By recognizing these patterns, algorithms can predict future price movements with a higher degree of accuracy than traditional methods. Imagine having a crystal ball that can tell you which stocks are likely to rise or fall in the coming months. AI-driven market analysis brings this vision closer to reality.

But the power of AI in market analysis goes beyond just predicting price movements. It can also help investors understand the underlying drivers of market trends. AI algorithms can analyze vast datasets to identify the factors that are influencing market sentiment, such as interest rate changes, economic growth, or political events. This knowledge can be crucial for making informed investment decisions, allowing investors to position their portfolios in line with anticipated market shifts.

AI-driven market analysis is not without its limitations. It's essential to remember that AI algorithms are only as good as the data they are trained on. If the data is biased or incomplete, the results will be unreliable. Furthermore, AI cannot predict the future with absolute certainty. Market movements are influenced by a myriad of factors, some of which are impossible to quantify. AI should be viewed as a tool to enhance investment decision-making, not a magic bullet that guarantees success.

However, the potential of AI in market analysis is undeniable. As the technology continues to evolve, we can expect to see even more sophisticated algorithms capable of extracting deeper insights from vast amounts of data. This will empower investors to make more informed decisions, navigate market volatility with greater confidence, and ultimately achieve their financial goals.

Imagine a world where financial information is readily available and understandable for everyone. This is the vision of AI-powered financial analysis, where sophisticated algorithms can analyze complex data, identify trends, and uncover investment opportunities. It's like having a personal financial advisor constantly working in the background, providing insights and recommendations tailored to your individual needs.

AI algorithms can analyze vast amounts of data, including historical market performance, economic indicators, news sentiment, and even social media trends. By recognizing patterns and relationships in this data, they can paint a picture of the market's current state and predict potential future movements. This ability to identify trends and anomalies that might escape human observation is what sets AI apart.

One of the most valuable applications of AI in financial analysis is its ability to personalize investment recommendations. AI algorithms can analyze an individual's financial profile, including their risk tolerance, investment goals, and time horizon. Based on this analysis, they can recommend specific investments that are likely to suit their individual circumstances. This level of personalized advice is often difficult to achieve with traditional financial advisors, who often rely on standardized strategies that may not be optimal for every individual.

Furthermore, AI can help investors understand the underlying drivers of market trends. By analyzing data from various sources, AI algorithms can identify the factors that are influencing market sentiment, such as interest rate changes, economic growth, or geopolitical events. This knowledge can empower investors to make more informed decisions, aligning their portfolios with anticipated market shifts and positioning themselves for potential gains.

AI is also transforming the world of portfolio management. AI algorithms can analyze portfolios in real-time, identifying potential risks and opportunities that might not be immediately apparent to human analysts. This allows investors to make dynamic adjustments to their portfolios, ensuring that they remain aligned with their investment goals and risk tolerance.

However, it's crucial to remember that AI is just a tool. While it can provide valuable insights and recommendations, it should not be solely relied upon for investment decisions. AI algorithms are only as good as the data they are trained on, and they cannot predict the future with absolute certainty. Ultimately, the responsibility for investment decisions lies with the individual investor.

The future of financial analysis is inextricably linked with AI. As the technology continues to evolve, we can expect to see even more sophisticated algorithms capable of extracting deeper insights from vast amounts of data. This will empower investors to make more informed decisions, navigate market volatility with greater confidence, and ultimately achieve their financial goals.

AI is not just revolutionizing the way we invest, it is also democratizing access to financial information and expertise. With AI-powered tools, individuals can gain insights and make decisions that were previously only available to professional investors. This is a powerful force for financial empowerment, enabling individuals to take control of their financial future and build wealth for themselves and their families.

In the age of AI, the financial landscape is constantly shifting. By embracing the power of AI, investors can gain a competitive edge, make more informed decisions, and navigate the complexities of the financial markets with greater confidence. This is the path to achieving financial freedom and securing a brighter financial future.

PERSONALIZED FINANCIAL RECOMMENDATIONS

Imagine a world where your financial goals are not just aspirations, but a carefully crafted roadmap guided by a personalized financial advisor. This advisor, however, is not a person but a sophisticated AI system, meticulously analyzing your financial profile and goals to deliver tailored recommendations. This is the realm of personalized financial recommendations powered by AI.

Personalized financial recommendations, powered by AI, are not just about algorithms crunching numbers; they are about understanding your unique financial landscape. AI can delve deep into your income, expenses, debt, assets, risk tolerance, and investment goals to provide a comprehensive picture of your financial well-being. Based on this data, it can tailor recommendations that align with your individual needs and aspirations.

One of the key advantages of AI-powered personalized financial recommendations is their ability to adapt and evolve with your financial journey. As your circumstances change, so too can your financial needs and goals. AI can continuously monitor your financial profile, adjust your portfolio as needed, and suggest new strategies based on changing market conditions and your own evolving aspirations. This dynamic approach ensures that your investment strategy remains aligned with your financial goals at every stage of life.

Let's consider a practical example. Imagine a young professional, Sarah, starting her investment journey. Sarah is looking to build a diversified portfolio that balances growth and stability. Using an AI-powered financial tool, Sarah can input her financial goals, risk tolerance, and investment horizon. The AI analyzes this information, taking into account her income, expenses, and existing assets. Based on this analysis, the AI suggests a personalized portfolio allocation, recommending a mix of stocks, bonds, and other assets that align with her risk profile and long-term goals.

As Sarah's income and expenses change over time, she can update her financial profile within the AI-powered tool. The AI will then recalculate her portfolio allocation, adjusting her investments accordingly. If Sarah's risk tolerance changes, for example, she can adjust this setting within the tool, and the AI will automatically modify her portfolio to reflect the new risk level.

The benefits of personalized financial recommendations extend beyond portfolio allocation. AI can also assist in:

- **Budgeting and Expense Management:** AI can analyze your spending patterns, identify areas where you might be overspending, and offer personalized budgeting tips to help you stay on track with your financial goals.
- **Debt Management:** AI can help you strategize to pay down debt more efficiently, potentially suggesting debt consolidation strategies or recommending the most beneficial ways to allocate extra payments.
- **Retirement Planning:** AI can project your future retirement income, analyze your current savings, and offer personalized retirement planning strategies to help you reach your desired lifestyle in retirement.
- **Tax Optimization:** AI can analyze your tax situation and identify potential tax deductions or strategies to optimize your tax liability.

The ability of AI to process vast amounts of data and identify patterns that humans might miss, makes it an invaluable tool for enhancing financial decision-making. By leveraging AI, individuals can gain a deeper understanding of their financial situation, make more informed investment decisions, and achieve their financial goals more efficiently.

However, it is important to note that AI is not a replacement for human judgment and financial expertise. While AI can provide valuable insights and recommendations, it's essential to understand the limitations and potential biases of AI systems. It's crucial to use AI as a tool to enhance financial decision-making, not as a substitute for your own financial understanding and due diligence.

Here are some additional points to consider about AI-powered personalized financial recommendations:

- **Transparency and Explainability:** It is important to choose AI-powered tools that offer transparency and explainability. Understand how the algorithms work and the reasoning behind their recommendations.
- **Data Privacy and Security:** Ensure that the AI tools you use have robust security measures to protect your personal financial data from unauthorized access.
- **Human Oversight:** Always maintain human oversight of your finances. While AI can be a powerful tool, it's crucial to be involved in the decision-making process and understand the rationale behind any recommended actions.

The future of personalized financial recommendations is bright. As AI technology continues to evolve, we can expect to see even more sophisticated and tailored solutions that empower individuals to take control of their financial futures. By embracing AI as a tool for informed decision-making, individuals can unlock a world of financial opportunities and achieve their financial goals more effectively.

AI FOR RISK ASSESSMENT AND PORTFOLIO OPTIMIZATION

Imagine a world where analyzing market data, assessing risks, and optimizing your investment portfolio doesn't require hours of tedious research and calculations. This is the power of AI in the realm of risk assessment and portfolio optimization. AI algorithms, trained on vast datasets of historical market data, can analyze complex patterns and predict potential risks with remarkable accuracy.

Think of it as having a seasoned financial expert, armed with supercomputing power, working tirelessly behind the scenes to analyze every nuance of the market. AI can evaluate a multitude of factors, including economic indicators, company performance, geopolitical events, and even sentiment analysis from social media, to identify potential risks and opportunities. This allows investors to make informed decisions based on a comprehensive understanding of market dynamics.

AI-Driven Risk Assessment: A Deeper Dive

AI's ability to assess investment risks goes beyond just analyzing historical data. Advanced algorithms employ sophisticated techniques like machine learning, deep learning, and natural language processing to identify patterns and anomalies that may not be evident to human analysts.

For example, AI can analyze news articles, social media posts, and other text data to gauge market sentiment and identify potential risk factors. A sudden surge in negative news about a particular industry or company could indicate a potential downturn, allowing investors to adjust their portfolio accordingly.

Moreover, AI can also assess the risk profiles of individual investors, taking into account their financial goals, time horizons, and risk tolerance. This allows for the creation of personalized investment portfolios that align with individual risk appetites.

Portfolio Optimization: AI as Your Investment Strategist

Once AI has identified potential risks and opportunities, it can help optimize your portfolio for maximum returns while minimizing risk. AI algorithms use complex optimization techniques to determine the ideal asset allocation based on your specific investment objectives.

For example, AI might recommend a higher allocation to growth stocks if you have a long-term investment horizon and a high risk tolerance. On the other hand, for investors with a shorter time horizon and a lower risk tolerance, AI might recommend a greater allocation to more conservative investments like bonds.

The Benefits of AI-Powered Portfolio Optimization

The advantages of AI-driven portfolio optimization are numerous:

- **Improved Risk Management:** AI algorithms can identify and mitigate risks that might be overlooked by human analysts, leading to more robust and resilient portfolios.
- **Enhanced Diversification:** AI can analyze vast datasets of historical data to create diversified portfolios that effectively spread risk across different asset classes.

- **Personalized Investment Strategies:** AI can tailor investment strategies to individual needs, ensuring portfolios are aligned with risk tolerance, time horizons, and financial goals.
- **Automated Rebalancing:** AI can automatically rebalance portfolios as market conditions change, ensuring that asset allocations remain in line with investment objectives.
- **Reduced Costs:** AI-powered tools can significantly reduce the costs associated with investment management, making professional financial advice more accessible.

AI-Powered Tools for Portfolio Optimization: A Glimpse

There are a plethora of AI-powered tools available for investors seeking to optimize their portfolios:

- **Robo-advisors:** These platforms use AI algorithms to provide automated investment advice and portfolio management services, typically at a fraction of the cost of traditional advisors.
- **Automated Trading Platforms:** These platforms use AI algorithms to execute trades based on predefined strategies, allowing for faster and more efficient execution.
- **Financial Modeling Software:** AI-powered software can create sophisticated financial models that simulate different market scenarios, allowing investors to test their strategies and understand potential outcomes.

AI for Risk Assessment and Portfolio Optimization: A New Era of Investing

AI is transforming the landscape of personal finance, empowering investors to make informed decisions and optimize their portfolios for success. By harnessing the power of AI, investors can navigate the complexities of the financial markets with greater confidence and achieve their financial goals.

However, it is important to remember that AI is a tool, not a magic bullet. While AI can provide valuable insights and automate many investment processes, it's essential to remain a proactive participant in your financial journey. Understand the limitations of AI, exercise critical thinking, and maintain a healthy balance between AI-driven insights and your own financial expertise.

The future of investing is a blend of human ingenuity and technological advancement, with AI as a powerful ally in achieving your financial aspirations. By embracing this new era of investment, you can unlock the full potential of your investment journey, empowering you to navigate the complexities of the financial markets with greater confidence and achieve your financial dreams.

CHAPTER 3

THE ETHICS OF AI IN FINANCE
THE BALANCING ACT

ETHICAL CONSIDERATIONS IN AI-DRIVEN FINANCE

The integration of AI into the financial realm has ushered in a new era of opportunities and challenges, demanding careful consideration of ethical implications. While AI promises enhanced efficiency, personalized services, and data-driven insights, its deployment raises crucial questions concerning fairness, privacy, and accountability. This section delves into these ethical considerations, examining the potential pitfalls and highlighting the need for responsible AI development and implementation in finance.

Bias in AI Algorithms: One of the most pressing concerns surrounding AI in finance is the potential for bias in algorithms. These algorithms are trained on vast amounts of data, and if this data reflects historical inequalities or societal biases, the AI system may perpetuate these biases in its decision-making processes. For instance, credit scoring algorithms trained on historical data could inadvertently discriminate against certain demographic groups based on past lending practices, leading to unfair access to credit.

To mitigate this risk, it is crucial to develop AI algorithms that are transparent, fair, and inclusive. Data scientists must carefully examine the data used to train AI models, identifying and addressing any potential biases. Techniques like data augmentation, fairness metrics, and explainable AI can be employed to ensure algorithmic fairness and minimize discriminatory outcomes.

Privacy Concerns in AI-Driven Finance: The increasing use of AI in finance raises significant privacy concerns. AI systems often collect and analyze vast amounts of personal data, including financial transactions, spending habits, and personal preferences. This data can be highly sensitive, and its misuse or breach could have severe consequences for individuals.

Ensuring data privacy and security must be a paramount priority in the development and deployment of AI-driven financial services. Strong data protection regulations, such as GDPR and CCPA, are essential to safeguarding sensitive information. Financial institutions and AI developers must implement robust data encryption, anonymization techniques, and access control measures to protect user data. Transparency regarding data collection, usage, and security practices is also crucial to build trust and foster responsible data stewardship.

Transparency and Explainability of AI Decisions: Another ethical challenge lies in the lack of transparency and explainability surrounding AI-driven financial decisions. Complex AI algorithms, often referred to as "black boxes," can generate highly accurate predictions but may not provide clear insights into the reasoning behind their decisions. This opaqueness can make it difficult for users to understand how AI is impacting their financial choices, leading to mistrust and a sense of helplessness.

To address this challenge, efforts are underway to develop "explainable AI" (XAI) techniques. XAI aims to make AI decisions transparent and understandable, allowing users to comprehend the reasoning behind an algorithm's recommendations. This transparency is crucial for building trust in AI-driven financial services and ensuring responsible decision-making. By providing clear explanations for AI-generated predictions, users can better assess the risks and opportunities associated with their financial choices, fostering informed decision-making.

The Importance of Human Oversight and Intervention: While AI has the potential to revolutionize finance, it is crucial to recognize that it should not replace human judgment entirely. Human oversight and intervention remain essential in financial decision-making, especially in complex and nuanced situations where AI may lack the necessary context or understanding.

Financial professionals should use AI as a tool to augment their decision-making processes, relying on their experience, judgment, and ethical considerations to guide their choices. This hybrid approach ensures a balance between the efficiency of AI and the wisdom and accountability of human expertise.

Ethical Considerations in AI-Driven Investment Decisions: The rise of AI in investment management raises specific ethical concerns. AI algorithms can analyze vast amounts of data, identify patterns, and predict market trends, but their reliance on historical data can create a risk of perpetuating past biases. If AI algorithms are trained on data that reflects past discrimination or market inefficiencies, they may inadvertently perpetuate these biases in their investment recommendations, potentially harming certain groups of investors.

It is essential to ensure that AI algorithms are trained on diverse and representative data, reflecting the full spectrum of market conditions and investor profiles. Regular audits and ethical assessments are crucial to identify and mitigate potential biases in AI-driven investment decisions. This includes exploring the potential impacts on different socioeconomic groups, considering factors such as income, gender, race, and location.

The Need for Responsible AI Development and Deployment: To address these ethical concerns, responsible AI development and deployment are crucial. This involves adhering to ethical guidelines, implementing robust data privacy measures, fostering transparency and explainability, and ensuring human oversight in decision-making.

Financial institutions and AI developers have a responsibility to develop and deploy AI solutions that are fair, unbiased, transparent, and accountable. This includes promoting diversity and inclusion in AI development teams, conducting thorough ethical assessments of AI algorithms, and actively engaging with stakeholders to address concerns and ensure responsible use of AI in finance.

The Future of Ethical AI in Finance: The future of ethical AI in finance is intertwined with advancements in technology, evolving regulations, and societal values. As AI continues to evolve, it is crucial to prioritize ethical considerations throughout the development and deployment process. Building trust and ensuring responsible AI adoption requires ongoing dialogue, collaboration, and a shared commitment to ethical principles.

Key Ethical Principles for AI in Finance:

- **Fairness and Non-discrimination:** AI systems should be designed and deployed in a way that prevents discrimination against individuals or groups based on protected characteristics.
- **Transparency and Explainability:** AI decisions should be transparent and explainable, allowing users to understand the reasoning behind them.
- **Privacy and Data Security:** Personal data collected by AI systems should be protected from unauthorized access, use, or disclosure.
- **Accountability and Responsibility:** Developers and users of AI systems should be held accountable for their actions and decisions.
- **Human Oversight and Intervention:** AI should be used to augment human decision-making, not replace it entirely.
- **Continuous Learning and Adaptation:** AI systems should be continually evaluated and adapted to ensure their ethical performance.

The Road Ahead: The ethical landscape of AI in finance is constantly evolving. As AI technology advances and its applications expand, it is essential to remain vigilant in addressing ethical considerations and promoting responsible AI development and deployment. By prioritizing ethical principles, fostering transparency, and ensuring human oversight, we can harness the transformative power of AI while safeguarding the integrity and fairness of the financial system.

The Potential Risks of AI in Investment Decisions

While the allure of AI in investment decisions is undeniable, a critical lens must be applied to acknowledge the potential risks. As with any powerful tool, relying solely on AI for financial decisions without human oversight can lead to unintended consequences and unforeseen vulnerabilities.

One significant risk lies in the inherent bias present in AI algorithms. These algorithms are trained on vast datasets, which may reflect existing societal biases, inadvertently perpetuating inequalities in investment outcomes. For instance, an algorithm trained on historical data might favor investments in sectors dominated by certain demographics, leading to a skewed allocation of resources.

Moreover, AI models can be susceptible to manipulation and hacking. Malicious actors can exploit vulnerabilities in algorithms, potentially leading to fraudulent transactions or manipulating market prices. This emphasizes the importance of robust security measures and ongoing monitoring to safeguard against such attacks.

Furthermore, AI algorithms can be opaque and difficult to interpret. The complex calculations and intricate decision-making processes within these algorithms can make it challenging to understand why a particular investment recommendation was made. This lack of transparency can hinder accountability and make it difficult to identify and address potential errors.

Another crucial concern is the potential for AI-driven "flash crashes". Rapid, automated trading decisions based on AI algorithms can amplify market volatility and lead to sudden and dramatic drops in asset prices. This underscores the need for human intervention and regulatory oversight to prevent excessive and potentially destabilizing market fluctuations.

Furthermore, the overreliance on AI can lead to a decline in human financial literacy and decision-making skills. If individuals become overly dependent on AI for financial guidance, they might lose the ability to analyze market trends, evaluate investment opportunities, and make independent financial decisions. This could create a dangerous dependence on technology, potentially hindering individual financial empowerment and financial independence.

It's essential to recognize that AI is a tool, not a replacement for human judgment and financial acumen. AI can provide valuable insights, enhance efficiency, and streamline investment processes. However, it should be used in conjunction with human expertise, critical thinking, and a thorough understanding of individual financial goals, risk tolerance, and market dynamics.

A robust ethical framework for AI in finance is paramount. This framework should prioritize transparency, fairness, accountability, and human oversight. Regulators, financial institutions, and developers must work together to establish clear guidelines and standards for the development and deployment of AI-powered financial tools.

The role of financial literacy becomes even more crucial in the AI era. Individuals must possess the skills to understand the intricacies of AI algorithms, critically evaluate investment recommendations, and make informed financial decisions. Financial education initiatives should focus on equipping individuals with the knowledge and tools to navigate the complexities of AI-driven finance and harness its potential responsibly.

The democratization of financial services through AI offers exciting possibilities, but it must be balanced with ethical considerations and a commitment to fostering financial literacy. AI can empower individuals with access to personalized financial advice, automated investment tools, and innovative financial products, but it's crucial to ensure equitable access and prevent the creation of new inequalities.

Ultimately, the ethical use of AI in finance requires a collaborative effort. Developers, financial institutions, regulators, and individuals must work together to ensure that AI technologies are used responsibly, ethically, and to the benefit of all. As we embrace the transformative power of AI in finance, it's crucial to proceed with caution, prioritize ethical considerations, and leverage its potential to create a more inclusive and equitable financial landscape.

The Importance of Financial Literacy in the AI Era

As we delve deeper into the realm of AI-driven finance, a crucial aspect emerges: the significance of financial literacy. This is not merely a passing notion; it's a critical pillar in ensuring responsible and effective navigation of the complex financial landscape shaped by AI. Just as a skilled navigator charts a course through turbulent seas, so too must individuals equipped with financial literacy steer their financial destinies in the ever-evolving world of AI-powered investments.

The rapid rise of AI in finance presents both incredible opportunities and potential pitfalls. AI algorithms can analyze mountains of data, identify patterns, and predict trends with remarkable accuracy. This leads to personalized financial recommendations, automated portfolio management, and a level of efficiency previously unimaginable. However, this power comes with a caveat: reliance solely on AI without a solid foundation of financial literacy can be a risky proposition.

Financial literacy serves as the bedrock for understanding how AI tools function, interpreting their outputs, and making informed decisions based on the insights provided. It empowers individuals to:

- **Discern the limitations of AI:** AI is not a magic bullet. It operates based on the data it's trained on, and its predictions are subject to inherent biases and limitations. Financial literacy helps individuals recognize these limitations and avoid placing blind faith in AI's outputs.
- **Evaluate the quality of AI-driven advice:** The financial services industry is increasingly populated by AI-powered robo-advisors and automated trading platforms. Financial literacy equips individuals to critically assess the quality of advice offered by these platforms, ensuring they align with individual needs and risk tolerances.
- **Understand the ethical implications:** AI in finance raises ethical considerations regarding data privacy, algorithmic bias, and the potential for unintended consequences. Financial literacy fosters an understanding of these issues, enabling individuals to

advocate for responsible and ethical AI development
and deployment in the financial sector.
- **Develop critical thinking skills:** AI can generate
impressive insights, but it's ultimately a tool. Financial
literacy promotes critical thinking skills, allowing
individuals to analyze AI-generated recommendations,
question assumptions, and make independent
judgments.

Imagine a scenario where an AI-powered investment advisor suggests a high-risk, high-reward investment strategy. A financially literate individual would ask critical questions: What are the underlying assumptions of this strategy? What are the potential risks and downsides? How does this align with my overall financial goals and risk tolerance? By applying critical thinking, individuals can avoid potentially disastrous outcomes, even when presented with seemingly compelling AI-driven recommendations.

Furthermore, financial literacy empowers individuals to leverage AI to their advantage. It enables them to:

- **Utilize AI tools for research and analysis:** Financial
literacy provides the framework for understanding the
data analyzed by AI algorithms. Individuals can use
this understanding to interpret AI-generated insights
and identify relevant trends.
- **Optimize their investment strategies:** Financial
literacy equips individuals to tailor AI-driven
investment strategies to their specific goals and risk
profiles. They can leverage AI algorithms to automate

portfolio management, rebalance assets, and make adjustments based on changing market conditions.

- **Access financial services more effectively:** AI has the potential to democratize access to financial services, making them more accessible and affordable for individuals from all walks of life. Financial literacy empowers individuals to navigate this evolving landscape, ensuring they utilize these services effectively and avoid potential pitfalls.

Financial literacy is not a static concept; it's a dynamic and evolving skillset. In the AI era, it becomes even more crucial as technology advances at breakneck speed. Individuals must embrace continuous learning, staying abreast of the latest AI developments and their implications for personal finance.

The world of finance is undergoing a profound transformation, and AI is at the forefront of this change. By equipping ourselves with financial literacy, we can navigate this new landscape with confidence and seize the opportunities it presents. We can harness the power of AI to achieve our financial goals, while remaining vigilant about the potential risks and ethical considerations. In this ever-evolving financial world, financial literacy is not just a choice; it's a necessity.

AI and the Democratization of Financial Services

In the realm of finance, access to information and expert guidance has traditionally been a privilege reserved for the wealthy. But the rise of AI is changing the game, ushering in an era of democratized financial services, where everyone has the opportunity to take control of their financial well-being.

AI's potential to democratize finance lies in its ability to break down barriers that have historically excluded individuals from accessing financial services. These barriers can include:

- **High costs:** Traditional financial advisors and investment services often come with hefty fees, putting them out of reach for many individuals. AI-powered solutions, on the other hand, can offer automated services at a fraction of the cost, making financial advice accessible to a wider audience.
- **Lack of knowledge and expertise:** Navigating the complex world of finance can be daunting, especially for individuals without prior experience or access to expert guidance. AI algorithms can provide personalized recommendations and insights, simplifying complex financial concepts and making them more understandable for everyone.
- **Geographic limitations:** Access to financial institutions and advisors can be limited in certain geographical locations. AI-powered platforms and tools can overcome these geographical limitations, providing access to financial services regardless of location.

Here are some specific ways AI is democratizing financial services:

- **Robo-advisors:** These AI-powered platforms provide automated financial advice and portfolio management services, often at a fraction of the cost of traditional advisors. Robo-advisors use algorithms to assess individual risk tolerance, investment goals, and financial situation, creating personalized investment portfolios. This accessibility allows individuals of all income levels to benefit from professional-grade investment management.

- **Microfinance and lending platforms:** AI is revolutionizing the way microfinance institutions and lending platforms operate, making it easier for individuals and small businesses to access loans and other financial products. AI algorithms can analyze vast amounts of data, including credit history, income, and spending patterns, to assess creditworthiness more efficiently and accurately. This allows institutions to extend loans to individuals who might otherwise be underserved by traditional financial systems.

- **Financial education and literacy:** AI-powered tools can provide personalized financial education resources, helping individuals learn about budgeting, saving, investing, and other essential financial concepts. Chatbots and virtual assistants can answer financial questions, provide guidance, and even offer interactive learning modules tailored to individual needs. This accessibility of financial education empowers individuals to make informed financial decisions and achieve their financial goals.

- **Financial inclusion:** AI can help bring financial services to underserved populations, including those in rural areas or those who lack access to traditional banking services. AI-powered mobile banking platforms and mobile payment systems provide a safe and convenient way to manage finances, even in remote areas with limited infrastructure. This promotes financial inclusion and allows individuals to participate in the financial system.

Real-World Examples of AI Democratizing Financial Services:

- **Acorns:** This robo-advisor app uses AI to round up purchases to the nearest dollar and invest the spare change in a diversified portfolio. It makes investing accessible to individuals who might not have the time or expertise to manage their own investments.
- **LendingClub:** This online lending platform uses AI to assess creditworthiness and connect borrowers with investors. By automating the lending process, LendingClub makes loans more accessible to individuals who may have difficulty obtaining traditional loans.
- **ZestFinance:** This company uses AI to create alternative credit scores, which can help lenders make more informed decisions about borrowers with limited credit history. This can expand access to credit for individuals who are traditionally underserved by traditional credit scoring systems.

The Ethical Implications of AI in Finance

While AI holds immense potential for democratizing financial services, it also raises ethical considerations. These include:

- **Bias in algorithms:** AI algorithms are trained on vast datasets, and if these datasets reflect biases, the algorithms can perpetuate those biases. This can lead to unfair lending practices, discriminatory investment recommendations, and other forms of financial inequality.

- **Data privacy:** AI algorithms rely on collecting and analyzing personal data, raising concerns about data privacy and security. It's crucial to ensure that personal data is collected and used ethically and responsibly.
- **Transparency and accountability:** AI decision-making can be complex and opaque, making it difficult to understand how algorithms arrive at their conclusions. This lack of transparency can raise concerns about accountability and the potential for misuse.

Navigating the Ethical Challenges

To ensure that AI benefits everyone, it's crucial to address the ethical challenges. Some key measures include:

- **Developing fair and unbiased algorithms:** By using diverse and representative datasets for training algorithms, we can minimize the risk of biases being reflected in AI decisions.
- **Implementing strong data privacy and security measures:** It's essential to protect personal data from unauthorized access and ensure that it's only used for its intended purpose.
- **Promoting transparency and accountability:** We need to develop mechanisms to understand how AI algorithms make decisions and hold developers and users accountable for their actions.

The Future of AI in Financial Democratization

AI is still in its early stages of development, but its potential to democratize financial services is undeniable. As AI continues to evolve, we can expect to see even more innovative applications in the field of finance. This includes:

- **Advanced personalization:** AI algorithms will become even more sophisticated, allowing for hyper-personalized financial advice and services tailored to individual needs and goals.
- **Increased financial literacy:** AI-powered education tools will become more interactive and engaging, making it easier for individuals to understand complex financial concepts.
- **Improved access to financial products and services:** AI will continue to break down barriers to access, providing financial services to individuals who are currently underserved by traditional financial institutions.

The democratization of financial services through AI holds immense promise for creating a more inclusive and equitable financial system. By addressing the ethical challenges and promoting responsible development and implementation, we can harness the power of AI to empower individuals to take control of their financial futures.

The Future of AI in Finance

As we stand on the precipice of a new era in finance, the potential of AI is as vast as the ocean itself. Imagine a world where your financial decisions are guided by algorithms that can analyze mountains of data, identify hidden patterns, and predict future market movements. This is not science fiction; it is the future of AI in personal finance, a future that is rapidly unfolding before our very eyes.

The next few years will witness a dramatic transformation in how individuals manage their money. AI will become an integral part of our financial lives, empowering us with tools and insights previously unimaginable. Robo-advisors, already gaining popularity, will become more sophisticated, offering personalized financial advice tailored to our individual needs and goals. They will adapt to changing market conditions, automatically rebalancing our portfolios to ensure optimal risk management.

But the impact of AI will extend far beyond automated portfolio management. The very way we access and understand financial information will be revolutionized. AI-powered tools will analyze vast amounts of data from diverse sources, providing us with comprehensive market insights, personalized recommendations, and detailed analyses of individual investments. We will have access to information previously available only to professional traders and analysts, empowering us to make more informed decisions.

Furthermore, AI will play a vital role in democratizing access to financial services. With the rise of AI-driven platforms, individuals will have access to financial advice and investment opportunities that were once only available to the wealthy. AI-powered tools can remove the barriers of high fees and limited accessibility, bringing financial empowerment to the masses.

However, this exciting future is not without its challenges. We must navigate the ethical considerations surrounding AI in finance, ensuring that its use is transparent, fair, and beneficial for all. The potential for bias in AI algorithms is a serious concern, and we must develop safeguards to prevent biased outcomes. Furthermore, protecting our financial data and privacy in the age of AI is paramount, requiring robust security measures and regulations.

The future of AI in personal finance is both exciting and daunting. It holds the potential to create a more equitable and accessible financial system, but only if we proceed with caution, addressing ethical concerns and ensuring responsible development and deployment. The key is to strike a balance between embracing the transformative potential of AI and safeguarding the integrity and security of our financial lives.

This is not just about technology; it is about shaping a future where individuals have the tools and knowledge to make informed financial decisions, empowering them to achieve their financial goals and build a more secure and prosperous future. The era of AI in personal finance is just beginning, and its impact on our financial well-being will be profound. By understanding the ethical considerations, leveraging AI responsibly, and embracing its potential, we can usher in a new era of financial empowerment for all.

The future of finance is not just about algorithms; it is about human ingenuity, resilience, and the unwavering pursuit of a brighter financial future for all. Let us embrace the transformative potential of AI while staying vigilant in navigating its ethical complexities, ensuring that this technology serves as a force for good in the financial world.

Chapter 4

Investing in Stocks

Navigating the Stock Market with AI

Understanding the Stock Market

The stock market, often referred to as the "Wall Street," is a complex and dynamic ecosystem where investors buy and sell shares of publicly traded companies. It's a fascinating world where economic forces, investor sentiment, and corporate performance intertwine to create a constant ebb and flow of prices. Understanding the stock market is crucial for anyone seeking to build wealth through investment.

Think of the stock market as a bustling marketplace where buyers and sellers come together to exchange ownership of companies. When you buy a share of a company's stock, you become a part-owner of that company, entitled to a portion of its profits and voting rights. The prices of these shares constantly fluctuate, influenced by factors like company performance, industry trends, economic news, and overall market sentiment.

There are two main types of stock markets:

- **The New York Stock Exchange (NYSE):** This is the world's largest stock exchange by market capitalization, where stocks are traded in a traditional, auction-based system.
- **The Nasdaq Stock Market:** This is a leading electronic stock market known for its focus on technology and growth companies.

Beyond these primary exchanges, numerous other stock markets operate globally, each with its unique rules and regulations.

Now, let's delve into the different types of stocks:

- **Common Stock:** This is the most common type of stock, representing ownership in a company and entitling holders to voting rights and potential dividends.
- **Preferred Stock:** This type of stock offers a fixed dividend payment and priority over common stockholders in the event of a company's liquidation. However, it generally doesn't come with voting rights.
- **Growth Stocks:** These stocks represent companies that are expected to experience rapid growth in earnings and sales, often in emerging industries. They tend to be riskier but offer potentially higher returns.
- **Value Stocks:** These stocks represent companies that are undervalued by the market, often due to temporary setbacks or a lack of investor attention. Value investors believe that these stocks have the potential to appreciate significantly as the market recognizes their true worth.

- **Blue-Chip Stocks:** These are stocks of large, well-established companies with a long history of profitability and dividend payments. They are generally considered less risky than growth stocks but may offer lower potential returns.
- **Penny Stocks:** These are stocks of companies with a very low share price, often associated with small or speculative companies. They can be highly volatile and carry significant risk.

Understanding the different types of stocks is crucial for making informed investment decisions. It helps you identify stocks that align with your risk tolerance, investment goals, and financial strategy.

How the Stock Market Works

The stock market operates through a complex interplay of supply and demand. When more buyers are interested in a particular stock, its price tends to rise. Conversely, when more sellers are eager to sell, the price tends to fall.

- **Brokers:** These are intermediaries who connect buyers and sellers in the stock market. They execute trades on behalf of their clients, ensuring that transactions are completed smoothly and efficiently.
- **Exchanges:** These are marketplaces where stocks are traded. They provide a platform for buyers and sellers to come together and determine prices.
- **Order Book:** This is an electronic system that lists all buy and sell orders for a particular stock, providing transparency into market demand and supply.

- **Market Makers:** These are specialized brokers who provide liquidity to the market by continuously buying and selling stocks, ensuring that trades can be executed quickly and efficiently.

Investing in Stocks: A Gateway to Wealth Creation

Investing in stocks can be a powerful way to build wealth over the long term. By owning shares of companies that are growing and generating profits, investors can potentially earn returns through both capital appreciation (increase in share price) and dividends (payments made by companies to shareholders).

However, it's essential to remember that investing in stocks involves inherent risks. Stock prices can fluctuate significantly, and there's always a chance of losing money. It's crucial to conduct thorough research, diversify your portfolio, and invest for the long term to mitigate risks and maximize potential returns.

AI's Role in Navigating the Stock Market

The rise of AI has revolutionized the world of finance, and the stock market is no exception. AI-powered tools are transforming how investors analyze data, identify opportunities, and make trading decisions.

- **AI-Driven Market Analysis:** AI algorithms can analyze vast amounts of market data, including historical price trends, company financials, news articles, and social media sentiment, to identify patterns and predict potential price movements.
- **Algorithmic Trading:** AI algorithms can execute trades automatically based on predefined rules and

strategies, eliminating emotional biases and enabling faster and more efficient decision-making.

- **Personalized Recommendations:** AI-powered platforms can provide personalized investment recommendations based on individual risk tolerance, investment goals, and financial profiles.
- **Portfolio Optimization:** AI can analyze investment portfolios and suggest adjustments to enhance diversification, minimize risk, and maximize returns.

Navigating the Stock Market with AI: A Practical Guide

AI can be a powerful tool for enhancing investment decisions, but it's essential to approach it with a discerning mind.

- **Don't Rely Solely on AI:** AI tools are valuable resources but should not be considered a replacement for human judgment and financial expertise.
- **Understand the Limitations of AI:** AI algorithms are based on historical data, and they may not always accurately predict future market movements.
- **Embrace Continuous Learning:** The field of AI is constantly evolving, and it's essential to stay abreast of the latest developments and refine your understanding of how AI can be leveraged for investment purposes.
- **Focus on Long-Term Investing:** AI can be a useful tool for short-term trading strategies, but it's essential to remember that long-term investing is the key to building sustainable wealth.

Conclusion: Embracing AI for Informed Investment Decisions

The stock market can be a daunting and complex world, but with the right tools and knowledge, it can be a powerful avenue for building wealth. AI is rapidly changing the landscape of finance, offering investors new and innovative ways to analyze data, identify opportunities, and make informed decisions. By understanding the fundamentals of the stock market, embracing the potential of AI, and making informed investment decisions, individuals can position themselves for long-term financial success.

AI-Powered Stock Analysis

Imagine a world where mountains of financial data are not just numbers, but whispers of future trends, hidden gems waiting to be unearthed. This is the world that AI, in its ever-evolving wisdom, is making a reality in the stock market.

AI algorithms, like tireless financial detectives, scour through vast amounts of data – from market trends and company financials to news articles and social media chatter – seeking patterns, anomalies, and insights that human eyes often miss. This data-driven approach transcends the limitations of human emotions and biases, providing a more objective lens to analyze stock performance and potential.

One of the most promising applications of AI in stock analysis is the identification of undervalued stocks. AI algorithms can identify companies with strong fundamentals but whose stock prices haven't reflected their true value. This is achieved by analyzing financial ratios, market sentiment, and other factors that contribute to a company's intrinsic worth. AI can then flag these undervalued stocks as potential investment opportunities.

Consider a scenario where a small-cap company has developed a breakthrough technology with vast market potential. However, due to limited market awareness or a recent setback, its stock price is languishing. An AI algorithm, trained on data from similar companies in the past, recognizes this pattern and flags the company as a potential "hidden gem" that could deliver significant returns if its true value is recognized by the market.

AI can also assist in predicting future stock performance. By analyzing historical data and current market conditions, AI algorithms can identify potential trends and forecast how a particular stock might perform in the future. This doesn't guarantee perfect predictions, but it can provide valuable insights that investors can use to refine their investment strategies and manage risk.

For instance, imagine an AI algorithm analyzing data on consumer sentiment, economic indicators, and industry trends. It identifies a surge in demand for electric vehicles, leading to an uptick in the stock prices of electric vehicle manufacturers. This information can then be utilized by investors to make informed decisions regarding their stock portfolio.

AI-powered stock analysis can also be used to create personalized investment recommendations. These recommendations are tailored to an individual's risk tolerance, investment goals, and financial situation. AI algorithms can identify stocks that align with these specific needs, providing a more personalized and effective investment experience.

The power of AI in stock analysis is not limited to identifying undervalued stocks or predicting future performance. It can also be used to refine trading strategies and optimize portfolio management. AI algorithms can analyze vast amounts of data to identify patterns and trends that can inform trading decisions. This can help investors make better-informed choices about when to buy, sell, or hold stocks.

AI can also help investors optimize their portfolio allocation. By analyzing risk levels and desired returns, AI algorithms can recommend the optimal mix of stocks, bonds, and other assets to achieve the investor's financial goals. This personalized approach can lead to more efficient portfolio management and improved investment outcomes.

However, it's important to remember that AI is a tool, not a magic bullet. While it can provide valuable insights and support informed decision-making, it's crucial to exercise caution and consider all aspects of an investment before making any decisions. AI algorithms can be influenced by biases in the data they are trained on, and they can also be vulnerable to unexpected market fluctuations.

Ultimately, AI is a powerful tool that can be used to enhance investment strategies, but it should be used in conjunction with human judgment and expertise. By leveraging the power of AI while retaining a critical perspective, investors can navigate the complexities of the stock market with greater confidence and potentially achieve better investment outcomes.

Imagine a scenario where an individual investor is considering investing in a particular company. They use an AI-powered stock analysis tool to review the company's financials, market sentiment, and industry trends. The AI algorithm identifies potential risks associated with the company's business model, such as increased competition or regulatory hurdles. Armed with this information, the investor can make a more informed decision, perhaps choosing to reduce their investment or even avoiding the company altogether.

This example highlights the importance of using AI as a complementary tool, not as a substitute for human judgment. By combining the power of AI with the wisdom of human experience, investors can navigate the complexities of the stock market with greater confidence and potentially achieve better investment outcomes.

The future of stock analysis is undeniably intertwined with AI. As AI continues to evolve, its ability to process data, identify patterns, and predict future trends will only become more sophisticated. This means investors who embrace AI will have a distinct advantage in navigating the ever-changing landscape of the stock market.

But the journey is not without its challenges. As AI becomes more powerful, it's crucial to address ethical considerations and ensure transparency and fairness in its applications. We must navigate the fine line between leveraging AI's potential and mitigating the risks associated with its use.

The story of AI in stock analysis is still being written, and its future is brimming with potential. By embracing the power of AI while maintaining a critical perspective, investors can embark on a journey of informed decision-making and potentially unlock the secrets of the stock market, one data point at a time. The future of investing is here, and it's powered by AI.

Automated Stock Trading Strategies

The realm of automated stock trading is where AI truly shines. Imagine a world where you set your investment goals, define your risk tolerance, and then let AI handle the intricate dance of buying and selling stocks, all while optimizing for potential profits. This is the promise of automated stock trading strategies, and AI is the driving force behind this revolution.

These strategies leverage sophisticated algorithms that analyze vast amounts of data – from historical stock prices and market trends to news sentiment and social media buzz. By identifying patterns and predicting market movements, these AI-powered systems execute trades based on pre-defined rules and parameters.

Types of Automated Stock Trading Strategies

There are various types of automated stock trading strategies, each with its own approach and risk profile. Here are a few prominent examples:

- **Trend-Following Strategies:** These strategies capitalize on the momentum of a stock by identifying trends and riding the wave. If a stock is consistently rising, the AI system might buy more shares, aiming to profit from its upward trajectory. Conversely, if a stock is trending downwards, the system might sell its holdings or initiate a short position.
- **Mean-Reversion Strategies:** This approach seeks to profit from the tendency of stock prices to revert back to their historical averages. If a stock is experiencing a temporary spike, the AI might sell, expecting it to fall

back to its mean. Similarly, if a stock dips below its average, the AI might buy, anticipating a rebound.

- **Arbitrage Strategies:** These strategies identify price discrepancies between different markets or assets. By taking advantage of these price differences, the AI system can generate risk-free profits by simultaneously buying and selling the same asset in different markets.
- **High-Frequency Trading (HFT):** This lightning-fast form of trading involves executing thousands or even millions of trades per second, taking advantage of minute price fluctuations. AI plays a crucial role in HFT, enabling algorithms to analyze data and execute trades faster than humans can ever hope to.

Advantages of Automated Stock Trading Strategies

Automated stock trading strategies powered by AI offer several advantages over traditional human-driven trading:

- **Speed and Efficiency:** AI algorithms can process vast amounts of data and execute trades at lightning speed, outpacing human traders. This allows them to capitalize on fleeting opportunities that human traders might miss.
- **Objectivity and Discipline:** Unlike humans, AI algorithms are not swayed by emotions like fear or greed. They adhere to pre-defined rules and parameters, ensuring objectivity and discipline in decision-making.
- **24/7 Operation:** Automated trading systems can operate continuously, monitoring markets and executing trades around the clock, even when humans

are asleep. This enables traders to capitalize on global market events and opportunities, regardless of the time of day.

- **Reduced Risk:** By following pre-defined rules and minimizing human intervention, automated trading systems can reduce the risk of emotional trading mistakes, which can lead to significant financial losses.

Risks and Considerations

While AI-powered automated trading strategies hold immense potential, it's crucial to be aware of the potential risks:

- **Algorithm Dependence:** Relying solely on AI algorithms can be risky, as they are only as good as the data they are trained on. If the data is flawed or incomplete, the algorithm's predictions can be unreliable.
- **Market Volatility:** Even the most sophisticated AI algorithms can struggle to predict sudden market shifts or unexpected events. These volatile situations can lead to unexpected losses, even with well-defined strategies.
- **Data Bias:** AI algorithms can be biased by the data they are trained on. This can lead to inaccurate predictions and potentially detrimental trading decisions.
- **Ethical Concerns:** The rapid pace and automation of AI-driven trading raise ethical concerns, particularly regarding transparency, fairness, and the potential for market manipulation.

The Evolution of Automated Trading

Automated stock trading has evolved significantly over the years. Early systems were relatively simple, relying on basic rules-based strategies. However, with the advent of powerful machine learning algorithms, AI has revolutionized the landscape of automated trading.

Modern AI systems can analyze vast amounts of data, including historical stock prices, market trends, news sentiment, and social media data. They use this information to identify patterns and predict market movements, allowing them to execute trades with greater precision and efficiency.

The future of automated trading lies in even more sophisticated AI systems that can learn and adapt in real-time. These systems will be able to factor in a wider range of data sources, including real-time news feeds, social media sentiment, and even economic indicators.

Tips for Using Automated Stock Trading Strategies

If you're considering using automated stock trading strategies, here are some tips to help you get started:

- **Start Small:** Begin with a small investment amount to minimize your risk while you learn the ropes.
- **Choose a Reputable Platform:** Select a platform with a proven track record and robust security measures.
- **Understand the Strategies:** Familiarize yourself with the different types of automated trading strategies available and choose one that aligns with your investment goals and risk tolerance.
- **Set Realistic Expectations:** Automated trading systems don't guarantee profits. Be aware of the

inherent risks and set realistic expectations for
potential returns.

- **Monitor Your Investments:** Regularly review the
performance of your automated trading system and
make adjustments as needed.
- **Seek Professional Advice:** If you're unsure about the
risks and benefits of automated trading, consult with a
financial advisor who specializes in AI-driven
investment strategies.

The Future of Automated Trading

The future of automated stock trading is bright. As AI technology continues to advance, we can expect even more sophisticated and intelligent algorithms that can analyze data more efficiently and execute trades with greater precision.

AI-powered automated trading platforms will become more user-friendly, making it easier for individuals to access these technologies and manage their investments. We can also expect to see the development of new and innovative trading strategies that leverage the power of AI.

However, it's crucial to remember that AI is a tool, and like any tool, it can be used for good or bad. As AI-driven trading becomes more prevalent, it's essential to ensure ethical and responsible use of these technologies.

By combining the power of AI with human intelligence and sound financial principles, investors can navigate the complexities of the stock market with greater confidence and unlock new opportunities for growth.

THE PSYCHOLOGY OF INVESTING

The realm of investing isn't just about numbers and charts; it's deeply intertwined with the human psyche. Emotions, like fear, greed, and impulsivity, can significantly impact our financial decisions, often leading to suboptimal outcomes. Understanding and managing these emotions is as crucial as comprehending financial ratios and market trends. This is where the psychology of investing comes into play.

Imagine yourself in a bustling marketplace, surrounded by vendors hawking their wares. You're drawn to a shiny new product, its price fluctuating wildly. One moment it's soaring high, tempting you to buy in, the next it's plummeting, causing you to panic and consider selling. This scenario mirrors the stock market, where emotions like fear and greed can drive impulsive decisions. Fear of missing out (FOMO) can lead to buying at inflated prices, while fear of losing money can prompt selling at a loss, locking in losses instead of riding out market fluctuations.

The concept of "cognitive biases" further emphasizes the role of psychology in investing. These biases are systematic errors in our thinking that can lead to irrational decisions. For example, the "anchoring bias" makes us cling to the first piece of information we receive, even if it's outdated or irrelevant. This can lead to investing in a stock based solely on its initial price, ignoring subsequent developments and analysis.

The "confirmation bias" reinforces our existing beliefs, leading us to seek out information that confirms our investment decisions while ignoring evidence to the contrary. This can result in ignoring warning signs about a company or market trend, leading to substantial losses. Similarly, the "herd mentality" causes us to follow the crowd, blindly investing in assets simply because others are doing so, without considering the underlying fundamentals or potential risks.

Mastering emotional decision-making requires developing emotional intelligence and discipline. The first step is to become aware of your emotional triggers and how they influence your investment decisions. Do you tend to get overly excited by market rallies or panic during downturns? Recognizing these patterns is crucial for taking control of your emotions.

Next, establish a clear investment strategy that aligns with your financial goals and risk tolerance. This strategy should guide your decisions, providing a framework for evaluating potential investments and making informed choices. This involves setting clear goals, conducting thorough research, and diversifying your portfolio across different asset classes.

Discipline is paramount in implementing your strategy. Resist the temptation to chase short-term gains or sell off assets in panic. Focus on the long-term vision and stay committed to your plan, even when the market throws unexpected curveballs. This requires patience, resilience, and a healthy dose of skepticism.

To further enhance your emotional intelligence, consider incorporating mindfulness practices into your investment routine. Mindfulness allows you to observe your thoughts and emotions without judgment, helping you to detach from impulsive reactions and make more rational decisions.

Imagine a seasoned investor, calmly observing market fluctuations without succumbing to fear or greed. This investor has cultivated emotional intelligence and discipline, allowing them to navigate market volatility with confidence. They understand the inherent risks and rewards of investing and have developed a strategy that guides their decisions.

Similarly, AI can play a valuable role in supporting your emotional well-being as an investor. By automating tasks, analyzing data, and providing personalized insights, AI can help to reduce stress, alleviate decision fatigue, and enhance your overall investment experience.

Consider an AI-powered platform that tracks your portfolio, alerts you to potential risks, and suggests rebalancing strategies based on your goals. This technology can act as a virtual advisor, reminding you of your long-term strategy and helping you stay focused on your financial goals.

However, it's crucial to remember that AI is a tool, not a replacement for human judgment. While AI can provide valuable insights, it's essential to understand its limitations and maintain a critical eye.

Finally, seek out a trusted financial advisor who can provide guidance and support. A good advisor will help you develop a customized investment strategy, provide objective advice, and help you stay on track through market upswings and downturns. They can act as a sounding board for your investment decisions, helping you to avoid emotional biases and maintain a balanced perspective.

Investing involves a delicate interplay between knowledge, strategy, and emotional discipline. By mastering your emotions and embracing the power of AI, you can navigate the complex world of investing with confidence, building a solid foundation for your financial future.

Building a Successful Stock Portfolio

Building a successful stock portfolio is the cornerstone of many investment strategies, and AI can be a powerful ally in this endeavor. While traditional methods often involve extensive research and analysis, AI-powered tools can streamline the process, providing valuable insights and automating key tasks.

Diversification: The Foundation of a Strong Portfolio

Diversification is the most important principle in investing. It's about spreading your investment across different asset classes and industries to reduce risk. Think of it like building a house: a well-diversified portfolio is like a house with strong foundations, walls, and a sturdy roof, making it less susceptible to damage from external shocks. A poorly diversified portfolio, on the other hand, is like a house built on shaky ground, vulnerable to collapse in the face of market volatility.

AI can be a valuable tool in achieving diversification. AI algorithms can analyze vast amounts of data to identify stocks that fit different categories, from large-cap growth stocks to small-cap value stocks, from healthcare to technology. This can help you build a portfolio that is well-balanced across different industries and market capitalizations.

Risk Management: Protecting Your Investment

Every investment carries some level of risk. It's impossible to eliminate risk entirely, but you can manage it effectively with a well-crafted investment strategy. AI can help you assess risk and mitigate it through advanced risk management techniques.

AI algorithms can analyze historical data to identify trends and patterns that might indicate potential risks. This can help you avoid stocks that are prone to volatility or that are experiencing financial distress. AI can also be used to construct investment portfolios that are tailored to your specific risk tolerance.

Identifying Growth Opportunities

AI can be a powerful tool for identifying growth opportunities in the stock market. AI algorithms can analyze vast amounts of data, including financial statements, news articles, social media posts, and even satellite imagery, to uncover hidden gems that may be overlooked by traditional methods.

For example, an AI algorithm might identify a company that is investing heavily in research and development or expanding into new markets. This could signal a potential growth opportunity. AI can also help you identify companies that are well-positioned to benefit from emerging trends, such as renewable energy or artificial intelligence itself.

AI-Powered Tools for Stock Selection

A number of AI-powered tools are available to help you select stocks:

- **Robo-advisors:** These platforms use AI algorithms to create and manage diversified portfolios tailored to your individual risk tolerance and investment goals. They can rebalance your portfolio automatically as market conditions change.
- **Automated trading platforms:** These platforms use AI algorithms to execute trades based on predefined strategies. They can help you take advantage of short-term market fluctuations or execute trades based on complex technical indicators.

- **AI-driven stock research tools:** These tools provide comprehensive insights into individual stocks, including fundamental analysis, technical analysis, and news sentiment. They can help you make more informed investment decisions.

Building Your Portfolio: A Step-by-Step Guide

Here's a step-by-step guide to building a successful stock portfolio with the help of AI:

1. **Define your investment goals:** What do you hope to achieve with your investments? Do you want to grow your wealth, save for retirement, or fund a specific goal like buying a house?
2. **Assess your risk tolerance:** How comfortable are you with market volatility? Are you willing to take on more risk for the potential of higher returns? Or do you prefer a more conservative approach with lower potential returns?
3. **Choose a diversified portfolio:** This means investing in a variety of stocks across different industries and market capitalizations.
4. **Research individual stocks:** Even with AI, it's important to do your own research on the companies you're considering investing in.
5. **Use AI tools for insights and analysis:** Leverage AI tools to gain a deeper understanding of the market, identify growth opportunities, and assess risk.
6. **Monitor your portfolio regularly:** Review your portfolio performance and make adjustments as needed.

7. **Stay informed:** Keep up with market trends and news that could impact your investments.

8. **Beyond Diversification:** While diversification is critical, it's not the only factor in building a successful stock portfolio. Other important considerations include:

    ○ **Value Investing:** This strategy focuses on finding undervalued stocks that are trading below their intrinsic worth. AI can help you identify value stocks by analyzing financial statements, industry trends, and other factors.

    ○ **Growth Investing:** This strategy focuses on finding companies that are growing rapidly and have the potential for high returns. AI can help you identify growth stocks by analyzing revenue growth, earnings growth, and other factors.

    ○ **Momentum Investing:** This strategy focuses on identifying stocks that are currently experiencing strong price momentum. AI can help you identify momentum stocks by analyzing price charts and other technical indicators.

A Word of Caution

It's crucial to remember that AI is just a tool, and it's not a replacement for sound investment judgment. While AI can provide valuable insights and help you make more informed decisions, it's important to exercise caution and use your own judgment when making investment choices.

Always be wary of investment schemes that promise unrealistic returns or that rely solely on AI to make decisions. Remember that no investment strategy guarantees success, and past performance is not necessarily indicative of future results.

The Future of Investing

The integration of AI into the realm of investing is just beginning, and it promises to revolutionize the way we manage our money. As AI technology continues to evolve, we can expect to see even more powerful tools and insights available to investors. This will empower individuals to make more informed decisions and achieve their financial goals with greater confidence.

The future of investing is bright with the potential of AI, but it's important to approach it with both excitement and a healthy dose of skepticism. By combining the power of AI with sound financial principles and a healthy dose of human judgment, you can navigate the stock market with confidence and build a successful portfolio that helps you achieve your financial goals.

CHAPTER 5

EXPLORING BONDS

A SAFER INVESTMENT OPTION WITH AI

UNDERSTANDING BONDS

Bonds, often referred to as fixed-income securities, represent a fundamental pillar of the investment landscape, offering a relatively safe and predictable return compared to stocks. Understanding bonds is crucial for any investor seeking to diversify their portfolio and manage risk effectively. In essence, a bond is a debt instrument representing a loan made by an investor to a borrower, typically a government or corporation. The borrower agrees to repay the principal amount of the loan, along with interest payments, at a specific maturity date.

The Anatomy of a Bond

Bonds come with several key characteristics that define their risk and return potential:

- **Face Value (Par Value):** This is the principal amount the borrower promises to repay at maturity. Bonds are typically issued with a face value of $1,000.

- **Coupon Rate:** The interest rate the borrower pays on the face value of the bond. This rate is typically fixed at the time of issuance and paid periodically (usually semi-annually).
- **Maturity Date:** The date when the borrower must repay the principal amount of the bond. Maturity dates can range from a few years to decades.
- **Yield to Maturity (YTM):** This represents the annual rate of return an investor can expect to receive if they hold the bond until maturity. It takes into account the coupon rate, the bond's current market price, and the time remaining until maturity.

Types of Bonds

The world of bonds is diverse, with various types catering to different investment objectives and risk tolerances:

- **Government Bonds:** Issued by national governments to finance public expenditures. They are generally considered very safe due to the backing of the issuing government. Examples include U.S. Treasury bonds, known for their low risk and liquidity.
- **Corporate Bonds:** Issued by companies to raise capital for expansion or operations. They typically offer higher yields than government bonds but carry more risk, as they are subject to the financial health of the issuing corporation.
- **Municipal Bonds:** Issued by state and local governments to fund infrastructure projects or public services. They offer tax advantages, as interest payments

are usually exempt from federal income tax and sometimes state and local taxes.

- **Zero-Coupon Bonds:** These bonds do not pay periodic interest payments but are issued at a discount to their face value. The investor earns a return by receiving the full face value at maturity.
- **Convertible Bonds:** These bonds can be exchanged for a specified number of shares of the issuing company's stock. They offer the potential for higher returns but also carry a higher risk.

Understanding Bond Risk and Return

Like any investment, bonds involve a trade-off between risk and return. Here's a breakdown of the key factors influencing bond risk:

- **Credit Risk:** The risk that the borrower will default on its obligations, failing to make interest payments or repay the principal at maturity. This risk is higher for bonds issued by companies with weaker financial performance or higher debt levels.
- **Interest Rate Risk:** The risk that the value of a bond will decline as interest rates rise. When interest rates rise, newly issued bonds offer higher yields, making existing bonds with lower yields less attractive.
- **Inflation Risk:** The risk that inflation will erode the purchasing power of the interest payments and principal repayment. If inflation rises faster than the coupon rate, the real return on the bond will be lower.
- **Liquidity Risk:** The risk that it will be difficult or costly to sell a bond before maturity. This risk is higher

for bonds issued by less well-known companies or bonds with unusual features.

Navigating Bond Investment with AI

In recent years, AI has emerged as a powerful tool for bond investors, enhancing decision-making, risk assessment, and portfolio optimization. Here are some key ways AI is transforming the bond market:

- **AI-Driven Bond Analysis:** AI algorithms can analyze vast amounts of bond data, including credit ratings, financial statements, market trends, and economic indicators, to identify undervalued bonds and predict future performance. This allows investors to make more informed decisions and potentially earn higher returns.
- **Bond Portfolio Optimization:** AI can help investors build diversified bond portfolios that align with their risk tolerance and investment goals. Algorithms can analyze different bond types, maturities, and credit ratings to create portfolios that are efficient and balanced.
- **Automated Bond Trading:** AI-powered trading platforms can execute trades automatically based on predefined strategies, allowing investors to capture market opportunities and manage their portfolios more effectively.
- **Real-Time Risk Management:** AI can monitor bond markets in real time, identifying potential risks and adjusting portfolio allocations as needed. This

proactive approach can help investors mitigate losses and enhance their overall returns.

- **AI and Bond Market Transparency**: The increasing use of AI in the bond market has also led to greater transparency and accessibility. AI-powered data analysis and reporting tools provide investors with comprehensive information about bond markets, allowing them to make more informed decisions. This transparency also helps to promote competition and reduce opportunities for insider trading.

Considerations for AI in Bond Investing

While AI offers tremendous potential in bond investing, it's essential to recognize its limitations and potential risks:

- **Data Bias:** AI algorithms are only as good as the data they are trained on. If the data is biased, the algorithms may produce inaccurate or misleading results.
- **Lack of Transparency:** The complex algorithms used in AI can be difficult to understand, leading to a lack of transparency and accountability.
- **Over-Reliance on AI:** Relying solely on AI for investment decisions can be risky. Human judgment and oversight are still essential to ensure that AI is used appropriately and ethically.

The Future of Bond Investing with AI

AI is poised to continue transforming the bond market in the coming years. Emerging technologies, such as machine learning and natural language processing, are expected to drive further innovation, leading to:

- **More sophisticated bond analysis:** AI will be able to analyze even larger datasets and identify more complex patterns, leading to more accurate predictions and better investment decisions.
- **Personalized bond recommendations:** AI will be able to tailor bond recommendations to individual investor profiles and investment goals, offering more personalized and customized investment strategies.
- **Increased accessibility to bond markets:** AI will make bond investing more accessible to individual investors by simplifying the process and reducing the need for specialized expertise.

Conclusion

Bonds remain an essential component of a well-diversified investment portfolio, providing a balance of risk and return. AI is revolutionizing bond investing, providing investors with powerful tools to make more informed decisions, manage risk effectively, and optimize their portfolios. By embracing the power of AI, investors can unlock new opportunities and navigate the complexities of the bond market with greater confidence. However, it's crucial to use AI responsibly, recognizing its limitations and potential risks while maintaining a critical and informed approach to investment decision-making. As the bond market continues to evolve, AI will undoubtedly play an increasingly pivotal role, shaping the future of this vital asset class.

AI-Driven Bond Analysis

Imagine a world where analyzing complex bond data, deciphering market trends, and identifying hidden gems in the bond market are no longer tedious tasks, but rather effortless processes powered by the keen eyes of artificial intelligence (AI). This is the exciting reality we are stepping into, where AI algorithms are revolutionizing the way we approach bond investments, opening up new opportunities and unlocking hidden potential.

AI's ability to analyze vast amounts of data with lightning speed and pinpoint patterns that humans might miss is a game-changer for bond investors. Imagine a scenario where you're considering adding a bond to your portfolio. Instead of wading through countless spreadsheets and market reports, you can leverage AI-powered tools to analyze historical bond data, predict future performance, and even identify bonds that might be undervalued by the market. AI can analyze factors like interest rate changes, credit ratings, economic indicators, and even geopolitical events to determine a bond's future potential.

Unlocking Undervalued Opportunities

At the heart of this AI-driven transformation lies the power of machine learning algorithms. These sophisticated algorithms are trained on massive datasets of historical bond information, allowing them to recognize complex relationships and identify trends that might elude human analysts. By analyzing historical patterns, AI can predict how bonds might behave under different market conditions, helping investors anticipate potential gains and risks.

For example, consider a bond issued by a company in a specific sector. An AI algorithm can analyze historical data to assess the company's financial health, its performance compared to its peers, and the overall health of the sector. This allows the algorithm to determine if the bond is priced fairly or if it presents a hidden opportunity. If the algorithm predicts that the bond's performance might be better than the market anticipates, it might flag it as an undervalued opportunity for investors.

Predicting Bond Performance

But AI's capabilities extend beyond simply identifying undervalued bonds. It can also predict the future performance of bonds, helping investors make more informed decisions. AI algorithms can assess economic indicators, interest rate trends, and even news sentiment to create predictive models of bond performance. This data-driven approach can help investors navigate the often-uncertain world of bond investments with greater confidence.

Think of it as having a crystal ball that helps you anticipate potential market shifts. AI can analyze news articles, social media trends, and even financial reports to gauge market sentiment and anticipate how it might impact bond prices. If AI predicts a potential downturn in a specific sector, investors can adjust their bond portfolio accordingly, potentially mitigating risks and preserving their investments.

Beyond Prediction: Portfolio Optimization

The application of AI in bond analysis goes beyond simple predictions. AI is also revolutionizing how we manage bond portfolios. By analyzing a portfolio's overall risk tolerance, diversification, and investment goals, AI can suggest adjustments that can improve the portfolio's overall performance.

This involves creating personalized recommendations tailored to an individual investor's financial needs and objectives. For instance, AI algorithms can analyze a portfolio and suggest specific bond types to diversify the portfolio, potentially reducing overall risk without sacrificing potential returns. This personalized approach ensures that investors are not simply investing in bonds blindly, but rather constructing a well-balanced portfolio that aligns with their unique circumstances.

The Human Touch Remains Crucial

While AI is a powerful tool for bond analysis and portfolio optimization, it's crucial to understand that it is not a replacement for human judgment and expertise. AI algorithms are excellent at processing data and identifying patterns, but they lack the human capacity for nuanced understanding and ethical decision-making.

As a financial advisor, I believe it is essential to blend AI's capabilities with my own expertise. I can use AI to analyze data, identify trends, and generate personalized recommendations, but I also rely on my experience and intuition to evaluate those recommendations and make final investment decisions. This collaborative approach ensures that the power of AI is harnessed responsibly and ethically, ultimately leading to better outcomes for my clients.

Navigating the Future of Bond Investing with AI

The future of bond investing is exciting, and AI is playing a pivotal role in shaping it. As AI technologies continue to evolve and become more sophisticated, we can expect even more innovative tools and strategies to emerge. These tools will enable investors to analyze bond data with unprecedented speed and accuracy, identify hidden opportunities, and manage their bond portfolios with greater efficiency and personalization.

However, as we embrace this AI-driven future, it's important to remember that AI is a tool, not a solution. It's essential to approach AI with a critical and discerning eye, ensuring that its use is ethical, responsible, and ultimately, aligned with our individual financial goals. By harnessing the power of AI while remaining grounded in our own judgment and expertise, we can navigate the future of bond investing with confidence, reaping the rewards of this transformative technology.

Bond Portfolio Management

Bond portfolio management is a crucial aspect of investing, particularly for those seeking a balance between risk and return. While stocks are known for their potential for high growth, bonds offer a more stable and predictable income stream, making them a valuable addition to any well-diversified portfolio. In the realm of bond portfolio management, AI tools are revolutionizing the way investors approach this asset class. AI algorithms can analyze vast amounts of data, identify trends, and predict future performance, empowering investors to make more informed decisions about bond investments. By leveraging AI, investors can optimize their bond portfolios, ensuring they align with their risk tolerance and investment goals.

Diversifying Your Bond Portfolio: A Foundation for Stability

Diversification is a fundamental principle of investment management, and it's particularly important in the context of bond portfolios. A diversified bond portfolio includes a range of bonds with different characteristics, such as maturity dates, interest rates, and credit ratings. This diversification helps mitigate risk by reducing the impact of any single bond's performance on the overall portfolio. Think of it as spreading your investments across different baskets, ensuring that if one basket takes a hit, others can help cushion the blow. AI algorithms can analyze various factors, including market conditions, interest rate trends, and credit risk, to recommend a diversified bond portfolio tailored to individual investor needs. These algorithms can assess the correlation between different bonds and select those that are least likely to move in tandem, further reducing portfolio risk.

Risk Management Strategies: Navigating Volatility

Risk management is an integral part of bond portfolio management. Investors need to carefully assess the risks associated with different bonds, considering factors such as interest rate risk, credit risk, and inflation risk. AI can play a significant role in risk management by analyzing historical data, market trends, and economic indicators to predict potential risks. For example, AI algorithms can identify bonds that are most susceptible to interest rate fluctuations, helping investors adjust their portfolios accordingly. They can also assess the creditworthiness of bond issuers, providing insights into the likelihood of default.

The Role of AI in Bond Portfolio Optimization

AI-powered tools can go beyond simply identifying risks and opportunities; they can actively optimize bond portfolios for maximum efficiency and return. These tools can analyze an investor's financial profile, risk tolerance, and investment goals to create a customized bond portfolio that aligns with their unique needs. AI algorithms can also adjust portfolios automatically based on market conditions, ensuring that they remain aligned with the investor's objectives. This dynamic adjustment helps investors take advantage of changing market conditions and potentially outperform passive investment strategies.

Real-World Examples: AI in Action

Let's explore some real-world examples of how AI is transforming bond portfolio management:

1. **Robo-advisors:** Robo-advisors are AI-powered platforms that offer automated investment advice and portfolio management services. These platforms typically use algorithms to create diversified portfolios based on individual investor profiles, including their risk tolerance and investment goals. Robo-advisors often incorporate bond investments into their portfolios, leveraging AI to manage these assets effectively.

2. **Automated trading:** AI is also revolutionizing bond trading. Automated trading platforms use algorithms to execute trades based on predefined parameters, eliminating the need for human intervention. These platforms can analyze market data in real-time, identify trading opportunities, and execute trades quickly and efficiently. AI-driven trading can be particularly advantageous in the bond market, where liquidity can sometimes be limited, and price movements can be rapid.

3. **Predictive analytics:** AI can also be used to predict future bond performance. By analyzing historical data, market trends, and economic indicators, AI algorithms can forecast potential price movements, interest rate changes, and credit risk. This information can help investors make informed decisions about buying, selling, or holding bonds.

Beyond Diversification: Adding Depth to Your Bond Portfolio

While diversification is essential, it's not the only factor to consider when constructing a bond portfolio. Investors should also consider the following aspects:

1. **Maturity dates:** Bonds have different maturity dates, indicating when the principal will be repaid. A portfolio with a mix of short-term and long-term bonds can help manage interest rate risk. AI algorithms can analyze the yield curve and recommend a maturity profile that aligns with the investor's risk tolerance and investment goals.

2. **Interest rates:** Bond yields are inversely related to interest rates. When interest rates rise, bond prices tend to fall, and vice versa. AI can help investors understand the relationship between interest rates and bond prices, allowing them to make informed decisions about bond investments.

3. **Credit ratings:** Credit ratings are assigned to bond issuers to reflect their creditworthiness. Higher credit ratings indicate lower risk, while lower credit ratings suggest higher risk. AI algorithms can analyze credit ratings and identify bonds with the desired level of risk.

The Future of Bond Portfolio Management: AI and Beyond

As AI technologies continue to advance, the bond market will likely see further innovation in bond portfolio management. Here are some potential future developments:

1. **Personalized investment advice:** AI could eventually provide personalized investment advice, tailored to an

individual's unique financial situation and investment goals. AI algorithms could analyze an investor's income, expenses, assets, liabilities, and other relevant data to create a customized bond portfolio that meets their specific needs.

2. **Enhanced risk management:** AI could become even more sophisticated in managing risk. AI algorithms could analyze a wider range of data, including social media sentiment, news articles, and economic forecasts, to identify potential risks that are not captured by traditional methods.

3. **Automated portfolio rebalancing:** AI could automate the process of portfolio rebalancing, ensuring that portfolios remain aligned with investor objectives as market conditions change. AI algorithms could analyze market data and adjust portfolios automatically, eliminating the need for human intervention.

Final Thoughts: Embracing AI for a Smarter Bond Portfolio

AI is transforming the way investors approach bond portfolio management. By leveraging AI-powered tools, investors can access more information, make more informed decisions, and optimize their portfolios for maximum efficiency and return. While it's important to remember that AI is a tool, not a magic bullet, it can be a valuable asset in navigating the complex world of bond investing. By embracing AI, investors can enhance their bond portfolios, reduce risk, and potentially achieve their financial goals more effectively. The future of bond portfolio management looks bright, and AI is poised to play an increasingly prominent role in shaping the landscape of this important asset class.

THE RELATIONSHIP BETWEEN STOCKS AND BONDS

The relationship between stocks and bonds is often described as a complementary one, and for good reason. While stocks represent ownership in companies and offer the potential for higher returns, they also carry greater risk. Bonds, on the other hand, represent loans to governments or companies and offer a more stable, predictable stream of income. By combining stocks and bonds in a diversified portfolio, investors can potentially mitigate risk while still achieving their financial goals.

Think of it like this: stocks are like the adventurous explorer, seeking out new territories and potentially striking gold. However, the journey is fraught with uncertainty and potential pitfalls. Bonds, on the other hand, are like the steady, reliable guide, providing a stable base and ensuring a safe return on the investment. Together, they can create a balanced and resilient team, capable of navigating the unpredictable terrain of the financial markets.

There are several key ways in which stocks and bonds can complement each other in an investment portfolio:

- **Risk Mitigation:** Bonds can act as a buffer against the volatility of stocks. When stock prices decline, bonds tend to hold their value better, providing stability to the overall portfolio. This diversification strategy helps reduce the overall risk and potential for losses.
- **Income Generation:** Bonds offer a predictable stream of interest income, which can provide a steady cash

flow for investors. This income can be used to meet expenses, reinvest in the portfolio, or simply provide financial peace of mind.

- **Inflation Protection:** While bonds generally offer lower returns than stocks, they can provide some protection against inflation. When inflation rises, interest rates tend to rise as well, leading to higher interest payments on bonds.

However, the optimal mix of stocks and bonds in a portfolio will depend on several factors, including:

- **Investment Goals:** An investor with a long-term growth objective might allocate a larger portion of their portfolio to stocks, while an investor seeking income and preservation of capital might favor bonds.
- **Risk Tolerance:** Younger investors with a longer time horizon may be more comfortable with higher levels of risk and allocate a larger portion to stocks. Older investors with a shorter time horizon may prefer a more conservative approach with a higher allocation to bonds.
- **Time Horizon:** The longer the investment time horizon, the greater the potential for stocks to outperform bonds. Conversely, shorter time horizons may call for a more conservative approach with a higher allocation to bonds.

AI can play a valuable role in helping investors determine the optimal balance between stocks and bonds in their portfolios. AI algorithms can analyze vast amounts of data, including historical market trends, economic indicators, and individual risk profiles, to provide personalized recommendations for asset allocation.

For example, AI-powered robo-advisors can create diversified portfolios that automatically adjust the allocation between stocks and bonds based on changing market conditions and investor preferences. These platforms use sophisticated algorithms to monitor market trends, track performance, and rebalance the portfolio as needed to maintain the desired risk and return profile.

Furthermore, AI can help investors identify specific stocks and bonds that align with their investment goals and risk tolerance. By analyzing data from various sources, including company financials, industry trends, and economic forecasts, AI algorithms can identify undervalued stocks with high growth potential or bonds offering attractive yields with low risk.

However, it is important to remember that AI is not a magic bullet. While AI can provide valuable insights and recommendations, it should not be considered a replacement for human judgment. Investors should always do their own research and consult with a qualified financial advisor to ensure that their investment decisions align with their personal circumstances and financial goals.

By embracing AI as a powerful tool, investors can gain a deeper understanding of the relationship between stocks and bonds and leverage its insights to build a diversified portfolio that meets their financial goals and risk tolerance.

AI and the Future of Bond Investing

The realm of bond investing, long considered a bastion of traditional financial practices, is experiencing a seismic shift as Artificial Intelligence (AI) enters the scene. This transformative force is ushering in a new era of innovation, efficiency, and enhanced decision-making, redefining how investors approach this asset class.

AI's impact on bond investing is multi-faceted, encompassing areas ranging from data analysis and risk assessment to portfolio optimization and market prediction. Its ability to process vast amounts of data at lightning speed, coupled with sophisticated algorithms, allows for a level of analysis and insight that was previously unattainable.

One of the most significant implications of AI in bond investing is its capacity to identify undervalued bonds. Traditional bond analysis often relies on manual processes, subject to human biases and limitations. AI, on the other hand, can sift through mountains of data, including economic indicators, credit ratings, and historical performance, to pinpoint bonds that are potentially overlooked by human analysts. This opens up new opportunities for investors to uncover hidden gems and potentially enhance their returns.

Moreover, AI is revolutionizing bond portfolio management. By analyzing individual investor profiles, including risk tolerance, investment goals, and time horizons, AI algorithms can construct highly personalized bond portfolios. This level of customization ensures that each portfolio is tailored to meet the unique needs and objectives of the individual investor. AI-driven portfolio management goes beyond simple diversification, employing sophisticated risk management techniques to mitigate potential losses and optimize returns.

Another area where AI is making waves is in predicting bond market movements. By analyzing historical data, economic trends, and geopolitical events, AI algorithms can identify patterns and signals that might indicate future shifts in bond prices. This predictive capability empowers investors to make more informed decisions, potentially timing their bond purchases and sales to capitalize on market fluctuations.

However, the rise of AI in bond investing is not without its challenges. One key concern is the potential for bias in AI algorithms. Since AI models are trained on historical data, they can inadvertently perpetuate existing biases present in that data. This could lead to unfair or discriminatory outcomes, particularly in areas such as credit scoring and bond risk assessment. It is crucial to ensure that AI algorithms are developed and used responsibly, with rigorous testing and ongoing monitoring to mitigate potential biases.

Another challenge is the need for human oversight and understanding. While AI excels in data analysis and pattern recognition, it lacks the human element of judgment, intuition, and empathy. It is important to remember that AI is a tool, not a replacement for human expertise. Investors should not solely rely on AI-generated recommendations without considering their own financial goals, risk tolerance, and overall investment strategy.

Despite these challenges, the potential of AI in bond investing is undeniable. As AI technology continues to evolve, we can expect even more sophisticated tools and applications to emerge. This will empower investors to make more informed decisions, potentially leading to higher returns, greater efficiency, and a more personalized investment experience.

Here are some examples of how AI is already shaping the future of bond investing:

- **Robo-Advisors for Bond Portfolios:** Robo-advisors, AI-powered platforms that provide automated financial advice and portfolio management, are increasingly offering bond investing options. These platforms leverage AI algorithms to analyze investor profiles and market conditions, constructing diversified bond portfolios that align with individual risk appetites and investment goals.
- **AI-Driven Bond Trading Platforms:** Several fintech companies have developed AI-powered trading platforms that specialize in bond markets. These platforms utilize sophisticated algorithms to identify trading opportunities, execute trades at optimal times, and manage risk throughout the trading process.
- **Machine Learning for Bond Risk Assessment:** Machine learning algorithms are being deployed to assess the creditworthiness of bond issuers. These algorithms can analyze vast amounts of data, including financial statements, market trends, and news articles, to predict the likelihood of default and provide more accurate credit ratings.
- **Predictive Analytics for Bond Market Trends:** AI-powered predictive analytics platforms are emerging to forecast bond market movements. By analyzing historical data, economic indicators, and geopolitical events, these platforms can identify patterns and trends

that may influence future bond prices. This information empowers investors to make more strategic decisions and potentially capitalize on market fluctuations.

As AI continues to transform the financial landscape, bond investing will undoubtedly be at the forefront of this revolution. By leveraging the power of AI, investors can gain a competitive edge, access new opportunities, and navigate the complexities of the bond market with greater confidence and precision. The future of bond investing is bright, driven by the innovative potential of AI and its ability to unlock new levels of efficiency, analysis, and personalization.

CHAPTER 6

REAL ESTATE INVESTMENT
UNLOCKING OPPORTUNITIES WITH AI

INTRODUCTION TO REAL ESTATE INVESTMENT

Real estate investment has long been a popular avenue for individuals seeking to build wealth and secure their financial future. It offers a tangible asset that can appreciate in value over time, providing both income and capital appreciation potential. However, navigating the complex world of real estate can be daunting, requiring a deep understanding of market trends, property valuation, and investment strategies.

Fortunately, the advent of artificial intelligence (AI) has ushered in a new era of opportunity for real estate investors. AI algorithms can analyze vast amounts of data, identify emerging trends, and provide valuable insights that can empower investors to make more informed decisions. By harnessing the power of AI, investors can gain a significant edge in a competitive market, unlocking opportunities that were previously inaccessible.

Benefits of Real Estate Investment

Real estate investment offers a multitude of potential benefits, making it an attractive option for investors of all levels of experience. Some key advantages include:

- **Tangible Asset:** Real estate provides a physical asset that can be seen and touched, offering a sense of security compared to intangible investments like stocks or bonds.
- **Potential for Appreciation:** Real estate values can appreciate over time, providing investors with the potential for significant capital gains. This appreciation can be driven by factors such as increasing demand, limited supply, and economic growth.
- **Income Generation:** Rental properties can provide a steady stream of passive income, helping to offset expenses and generate cash flow.
- **Tax Advantages:** Real estate investments often come with tax benefits, such as deductions for mortgage interest, property taxes, and depreciation. These benefits can significantly reduce an investor's tax liability.
- **Inflation Hedge:** Real estate can serve as an inflation hedge, as its value tends to rise along with inflation.

Challenges of Real Estate Investment

While real estate investment offers many potential benefits, it also comes with inherent challenges that investors need to be aware of:

- **High Entry Costs:** Real estate investments often require significant capital upfront, including down payments, closing costs, and ongoing expenses like property taxes and maintenance.

- **Illiquidity:** Real estate can be relatively illiquid, meaning it can be difficult to sell quickly if needed. This can make it challenging to access funds for emergencies or other investments.
- **Market Volatility:** Real estate markets can be subject to fluctuations, influenced by factors such as economic downturns, interest rate changes, and local market conditions.
- **Property Management:** Owning rental properties requires ongoing management responsibilities, including finding tenants, collecting rent, addressing maintenance issues, and complying with local regulations.
- **Financial Risk:** Real estate investments carry financial risks, such as the potential for property damage, tenant default, and changes in market conditions.

AI-Powered Real Estate Investment: A Strategic Approach

AI is revolutionizing real estate investment, offering investors tools and insights that were previously unimaginable. By leveraging AI, investors can gain a competitive advantage in navigating the complex and ever-evolving real estate market.

- **Data-Driven Decision-Making:** AI algorithms can analyze vast amounts of real estate data, including property records, market trends, and economic indicators. This data-driven approach allows investors to make more informed and objective decisions, reducing reliance on intuition or limited information.

- **Property Valuation:** AI can be used to accurately value properties, taking into account a multitude of factors, such as location, size, condition, and recent comparable sales. This can help investors make more precise assessments of fair market value, ensuring they are not overpaying for properties.
- **Market Trend Analysis:** AI algorithms can identify emerging trends in the real estate market, such as shifting demographics, economic growth patterns, and changes in consumer preferences. This knowledge allows investors to capitalize on emerging opportunities and avoid areas that are facing decline.
- **Investment Strategy Optimization:** AI can help investors develop and optimize their real estate investment strategies, factoring in their individual risk tolerance, investment goals, and financial constraints. AI-powered algorithms can suggest optimal property types, locations, and investment approaches based on a thorough analysis of the investor's profile and market conditions.
- **Automated Property Management:** AI-powered tools can automate many aspects of property management, from tenant screening and rent collection to maintenance scheduling and communication. This can save investors valuable time and resources, allowing them to focus on more strategic aspects of their investments.

Examples of AI in Real Estate Investment

The real estate industry is embracing AI at an accelerating pace, with numerous examples of its application in various aspects of the investment process. Here are a few notable examples:

- **AI-powered Real Estate Platforms:** Companies like Zillow, Redfin, and Trulia leverage AI algorithms to provide comprehensive property listings, market insights, and automated valuation tools. These platforms empower buyers and sellers with data-driven decision-making capabilities.
- **Automated Property Management Software:** Software like Buildium and AppFolio utilize AI to streamline property management tasks, automating tenant screening, rent collection, and maintenance requests. This frees up landlords and property managers to focus on more strategic initiatives.
- **Predictive Analytics for Market Trends:** AI-powered analytics platforms can analyze historical real estate data to identify trends, predict future price movements, and pinpoint areas with high growth potential. This information can help investors make strategic decisions about where and when to invest.
- **Automated Investing Strategies:** AI-driven robo-advisors are emerging in the real estate investment space, offering automated portfolio management services based on individual investment goals and risk tolerance. These platforms utilize algorithms to select and allocate real estate assets based on specific criteria, simplifying the investment process for busy individuals.

Ethical Considerations in AI-Driven Real Estate

As with any emerging technology, the use of AI in real estate investment comes with ethical considerations that need to be addressed. Some key concerns include:

- **Bias and Discrimination:** AI algorithms are trained on data sets that may contain biases, which could lead to discriminatory outcomes in the allocation of real estate assets or the provision of services. It is crucial to ensure that AI systems are developed and implemented in a fair and equitable manner, avoiding biases that could perpetuate existing inequalities.
- **Privacy and Data Security:** AI relies heavily on data, raising concerns about privacy and data security. It is essential to protect sensitive personal information and ensure that data is used responsibly and ethically.
- **Transparency and Explainability:** AI systems can be complex, making it difficult to understand how they arrive at their decisions. Transparency and explainability are crucial for building trust and accountability in AI-driven real estate investments.
- **Job Displacement:** The automation of tasks through AI could lead to job displacement in the real estate industry. It is essential to consider the impact on human workers and explore ways to mitigate potential job losses through retraining and upskilling programs.

The Future of Real Estate Investment with AI

AI is poised to continue transforming the real estate industry in profound ways, creating new opportunities and challenges for investors. Here are some potential future trends:

- **Hyper-Personalized Investment Strategies:** AI will enable investors to create highly personalized investment strategies that align perfectly with their individual needs, goals, and risk tolerance.
- **Increased Automation:** More tasks in the real estate investment process will be automated, from property valuation and market analysis to tenant screening and rent collection.
- **Smart Homes and Buildings:** AI-powered smart homes and buildings will become increasingly common, offering investors opportunities to generate additional income through rental premiums and energy efficiency savings.
- **Data-Driven Real Estate Development:** AI will play a vital role in real estate development, helping developers identify ideal locations, optimize building designs, and predict market demand.
- **Blockchain and Digital Real Estate:** Blockchain technology will enable the creation of digital real estate assets, offering investors new ways to invest in fractional ownership, fractional ownership, and tokenize properties.

Conclusion

The integration of AI into real estate investment is a paradigm shift that is opening up a new era of opportunity for individuals seeking to build wealth and secure their financial future. AI offers a data-driven approach to investment decisions, empowering investors with insights and tools that were previously inaccessible. By embracing AI, investors can navigate the complexities of the real estate market with confidence, optimizing their strategies and maximizing their returns. However, it is essential to be aware of the ethical considerations surrounding AI and ensure that its use is responsible and beneficial for all stakeholders. As AI continues to evolve and integrate further into the real estate industry, its impact on investors will continue to grow, shaping the future of real estate investment in profound ways.

AI-Driven Real Estate Market Analysis

Real estate investment has long been a popular avenue for individuals seeking to build wealth and secure their financial future. It offers a tangible asset that can appreciate in value over time, providing both income and capital appreciation potential. However, navigating the complex world of real estate can be daunting, requiring a deep understanding of market trends, property valuation, and investment strategies.

Fortunately, the advent of artificial intelligence (AI) has ushered in a new era of opportunity for real estate investors. AI algorithms can analyze vast amounts of data, identify emerging trends, and provide valuable insights that can empower investors to make more informed decisions. By harnessing the power of AI, investors can gain a significant edge in a competitive market, unlocking opportunities that were previously inaccessible.

Benefits of Real Estate Investment

Real estate investment offers a multitude of potential benefits, making it an attractive option for investors of all levels of experience. Some key advantages include:

- **Tangible Asset:** Real estate provides a physical asset that can be seen and touched, offering a sense of security compared to intangible investments like stocks or bonds.
- **Potential for Appreciation:** Real estate values can appreciate over time, providing investors with the potential for significant capital gains. This appreciation can be driven by factors such as increasing demand, limited supply, and economic growth.
- **Income Generation:** Rental properties can provide a steady stream of passive income, helping to offset expenses and generate cash flow.
- **Tax Advantages:** Real estate investments often come with tax benefits, such as deductions for mortgage interest, property taxes, and depreciation. These benefits can significantly reduce an investor's tax liability.
- **Inflation Hedge:** Real estate can serve as an inflation hedge, as its value tends to rise along with inflation.

Challenges of Real Estate Investment

While real estate investment offers many potential benefits, it also comes with inherent challenges that investors need to be aware of:

- **High Entry Costs:** Real estate investments often require significant capital upfront, including down payments, closing costs, and ongoing expenses like property taxes and maintenance.
- **Illiquidity:** Real estate can be relatively illiquid, meaning it can be difficult to sell quickly if needed.

This can make it challenging to access funds for emergencies or other investments.

- **Market Volatility:** Real estate markets can be subject to fluctuations, influenced by factors such as economic downturns, interest rate changes, and local market conditions.
- **Property Management:** Owning rental properties requires ongoing management responsibilities, including finding tenants, collecting rent, addressing maintenance issues, and complying with local regulations.
- **Financial Risk:** Real estate investments carry financial risks, such as the potential for property damage, tenant default, and changes in market conditions.

AI-Powered Real Estate Investment: A Strategic Approach

AI is revolutionizing real estate investment, offering investors tools and insights that were previously unimaginable. By leveraging AI, investors can gain a competitive advantage in navigating the complex and ever-evolving real estate market.

- **Data-Driven Decision-Making:** AI algorithms can analyze vast amounts of real estate data, including property records, market trends, and economic indicators. This data-driven approach allows investors to make more informed and objective decisions, reducing reliance on intuition or limited information.
- **Property Valuation:** AI can be used to accurately value properties, taking into account a multitude of factors, such as location, size, condition, and recent comparable sales. This can help investors make more

precise assessments of fair market value, ensuring they are not overpaying for properties.

- **Market Trend Analysis:** AI algorithms can identify emerging trends in the real estate market, such as shifting demographics, economic growth patterns, and changes in consumer preferences. This knowledge allows investors to capitalize on emerging opportunities and avoid areas that are facing decline.

- **Investment Strategy Optimization:** AI can help investors develop and optimize their real estate investment strategies, factoring in their individual risk tolerance, investment goals, and financial constraints. AI-powered algorithms can suggest optimal property types, locations, and investment approaches based on a thorough analysis of the investor's profile and market conditions.

- **Automated Property Management:** AI-powered tools can automate many aspects of property management, from tenant screening and rent collection to maintenance scheduling and communication. This can save investors valuable time and resources, allowing them to focus on more strategic aspects of their investments.

Examples of AI in Real Estate Investment

The real estate industry is embracing AI at an accelerating pace, with numerous examples of its application in various aspects of the investment process. Here are a few notable examples:

- **AI-powered Real Estate Platforms:** Companies like Zillow, Redfin, and Trulia leverage AI algorithms to provide comprehensive property listings, market insights, and automated valuation tools. These platforms empower buyers and sellers with data-driven decision-making capabilities.

- **Automated Property Management Software:** Software like Buildium and AppFolio utilize AI to streamline property management tasks, automating tenant screening, rent collection, and maintenance requests. This frees up landlords and property managers to focus on more strategic initiatives.
- **Predictive Analytics for Market Trends:** AI-powered analytics platforms can analyze historical real estate data to identify trends, predict future price movements, and pinpoint areas with high growth potential. This information can help investors make strategic decisions about where and when to invest.
- **Automated Investing Strategies:** AI-driven robo-advisors are emerging in the real estate investment space, offering automated portfolio management services based on individual investment goals and risk tolerance. These platforms utilize algorithms to select and allocate real estate assets based on specific criteria, simplifying the investment process for busy individuals.

Ethical Considerations in AI-Driven Real Estate

As with any emerging technology, the use of AI in real estate investment comes with ethical considerations that need to be addressed. Some key concerns include:

- **Bias and Discrimination:** AI algorithms are trained on data sets that may contain biases, which could lead to discriminatory outcomes in the allocation of real estate assets or the provision of services. It is crucial to ensure that AI systems are developed and implemented in a fair and equitable manner, avoiding biases that could perpetuate existing inequalities.
- **Privacy and Data Security:** AI relies heavily on data, raising concerns about privacy and data security. It is essential to protect sensitive personal information and ensure that data is used responsibly and ethically.
- **Transparency and Explainability:** AI systems can be complex, making it difficult to understand how they arrive at their decisions. Transparency and explainability are crucial for building trust and accountability in AI-driven real estate investments.
- **Job Displacement:** The automation of tasks through AI could lead to job displacement in the real estate industry. It is essential to consider the impact on human workers and explore ways to mitigate potential job losses through retraining and upskilling programs.

The Future of Real Estate Investment with AI

AI is poised to continue transforming the real estate industry in profound ways, creating new opportunities and challenges for investors. Here are some potential future trends:

- **Hyper-Personalized Investment Strategies:** AI will enable investors to create highly personalized investment strategies that align perfectly with their individual needs, goals, and risk tolerance.

- **Increased Automation:** More tasks in the real estate investment process will be automated, from property valuation and market analysis to tenant screening and rent collection.
- **Smart Homes and Buildings:** AI-powered smart homes and buildings will become increasingly common, offering investors opportunities to generate additional income through rental premiums and energy efficiency savings.
- **Data-Driven Real Estate Development:** AI will play a vital role in real estate development, helping developers identify ideal locations, optimize building designs, and predict market demand.
- **Blockchain and Digital Real Estate:** Blockchain technology will enable the creation of digital real estate assets, offering investors new ways to invest in fractional ownership, fractional ownership, and tokenize properties.

CONCLUSION

The integration of AI into real estate investment is a paradigm shift that is opening up a new era of opportunity for individuals seeking to build wealth and secure their financial future. AI offers a data-driven approach to investment decisions, empowering investors with insights and tools that were previously inaccessible. By embracing AI, investors can navigate the complexities of the real estate market with confidence, optimizing their strategies and maximizing their returns. However, it is essential to be aware of the ethical considerations surrounding AI and ensure that its use is responsible and beneficial for all stakeholders. As AI continues to evolve and integrate further into the real estate industry, its impact on investors will continue to grow, shaping the future of real estate investment in profound ways.

AI FOR PROPERTY VALUATION

magine a world where determining the true value of a property is as simple as feeding data into a sophisticated computer program. This is the reality that AI is bringing to the realm of real estate valuation. Gone are the days of relying solely on human appraisals, with their inherent subjectivity and potential for error. AI is ushering in a new era of precision and efficiency, transforming how we assess property values.

AI algorithms, trained on vast datasets of property transactions, market trends, and economic indicators, can analyze numerous factors that influence property value. These factors include location, size, age, condition, amenities, nearby schools, and even crime rates. AI can analyze these factors with a speed and accuracy that far surpasses human capabilities.

One of the key advantages of AI in property valuation is its ability to identify hidden patterns and trends that might escape human observation. By analyzing a vast amount of data, AI can uncover subtle market shifts, neighborhood demographics, and even the impact of local infrastructure projects on property values. These insights can be invaluable for both buyers and sellers, allowing them to make more informed decisions.

Furthermore, AI can eliminate bias from the valuation process. Traditional appraisals can be influenced by personal opinions, emotions, or even unconscious biases. AI, on the other hand, operates purely based on data and algorithms, ensuring objectivity and fairness in the valuation process. This is particularly important in a market where properties are often subject to speculation or emotional valuations.

AI-powered valuation tools are already making significant waves in the real estate industry. Many online platforms and real estate agencies are integrating AI-driven valuation models into their services, providing users with instant and accurate estimates of property values. These tools are proving to be incredibly helpful for buyers, sellers, and even investors who need a quick and reliable way to assess property values.

Beyond its ability to assess property values, AI is also revolutionizing the way real estate transactions are conducted. AI-powered chatbots are becoming increasingly common, providing instant responses to customer inquiries, scheduling appointments, and even negotiating offers. AI-driven platforms are streamlining the entire buying and selling process, making it more efficient and convenient for everyone involved.

The impact of AI on real estate valuation is not without its challenges. Some concerns include the potential for errors in AI algorithms, the need for data privacy and security, and the potential for job displacement in the real estate appraisal industry. However, these challenges are not insurmountable. Continued advancements in AI technology and the development of ethical guidelines can address these concerns and pave the way for a more transparent and efficient real estate market.

Here are some specific examples of how AI is revolutionizing property valuation:

- **Automated Valuation Models (AVMs):** These
  models use machine learning algorithms to analyze

property data, market trends, and other relevant factors to provide automated property valuations. AVMs are becoming increasingly sophisticated and accurate, offering a valuable tool for both buyers and sellers.

- **Comparative Market Analysis (CMA):** AI-powered CMAs can analyze recent sales data, active listings, and pending sales to provide a detailed picture of the current market conditions and the estimated value of a property.
- **Predictive Analytics:** AI can use historical data to predict future property values, allowing investors to identify potential investment opportunities and capitalize on market trends.
- **Property Inspection Automation:** AI-powered drones and other technologies can be used to perform property inspections, generating detailed reports that highlight potential issues and provide valuable insights for both buyers and sellers.
- **Real Estate Investment Analysis:** AI can analyze investment opportunities, calculate potential returns, and identify risks, providing investors with valuable insights for making informed investment decisions.

The integration of AI into real estate valuation is not just a technological advancement but a fundamental shift in the industry. AI empowers both buyers and sellers with the knowledge they need to make informed decisions, promoting a more efficient and transparent real estate market. As AI technology continues to evolve, we can expect even more transformative innovations in property valuation, further revolutionizing the way we buy, sell, and invest in real estate.

AI-Powered Real Estate Investment Strategies

he realm of real estate, long a bastion of traditional methods and human intuition, is now being reshaped by the intelligent automation of AI. This technological shift is opening up a world of unprecedented opportunities for investors, both seasoned and novice, seeking to maximize returns and mitigate risks.

AI's ability to analyze vast amounts of data, uncover hidden patterns, and predict market trends with remarkable accuracy is revolutionizing how we approach real estate investment. Gone are the days of relying solely on gut feelings and limited market insights. AI-powered tools are empowering investors with data-driven decisions, leading to more informed strategies and potentially higher returns.

One of the most significant ways AI is transforming real estate investment is through its ability to analyze market trends and identify lucrative opportunities. Traditional methods often relied on subjective assessments and limited data points, leading to potential biases and missed opportunities. AI, on the other hand, can sift through massive datasets, encompassing market data, property records, economic indicators, and even social media trends, to identify emerging patterns and pinpoint areas with high potential for growth.

Imagine an investor seeking to capitalize on the burgeoning demand for urban living in a specific city. Instead of relying on anecdotal evidence or limited market research, they could leverage AI to analyze historical property data, population growth trends, infrastructure development plans, and even local job market statistics. By analyzing this vast array of information, the AI algorithm could pinpoint specific neighborhoods or micro-markets within the city experiencing a surge in demand, enabling the investor to make strategic decisions about where to invest.

Furthermore, AI is transforming the way we assess property value. Traditional valuation methods often relied on subjective opinions and comparisons to similar properties, potentially leading to inaccuracies and biases. AI, however, can leverage advanced algorithms and machine learning models to analyze thousands of property data points, including location, size, condition, amenities, and recent sales data, to generate highly precise and objective valuations.

Imagine an investor considering purchasing a property in a rapidly developing area. Using AI-powered valuation tools, they can access a comprehensive analysis of comparable properties, recent market trends, and even factors like proximity to schools, transportation hubs, and local amenities. This comprehensive data-driven evaluation allows them to make a more informed decision about the fair market value of the property and negotiate a price that reflects its true worth.

AI is also revolutionizing the way we invest in rental properties. By analyzing historical data on rental income, vacancy rates, and neighborhood demographics, AI algorithms can predict future rental yields with greater accuracy. This allows investors to identify properties with the potential for high rental income and minimize the risk of vacancy.

AI can also assist in streamlining property management tasks, such as tenant screening, rent collection, and maintenance scheduling. By automating these processes, landlords can save time and resources while ensuring efficient and effective property management.

Beyond analyzing market data and predicting trends, AI is also transforming the way we finance real estate investments. AI-powered loan origination platforms are leveraging advanced algorithms to automate the loan application process, making it faster, more efficient, and potentially more accessible to a wider range of borrowers.

AI is also playing a significant role in the development of innovative real estate investment strategies. AI-powered investment platforms are offering sophisticated algorithms that can analyze a vast range of factors, including market trends, property data, and investor risk profiles, to recommend personalized investment portfolios tailored to individual goals and risk tolerance.

However, it's crucial to recognize that AI is not a magic bullet for real estate investment. While AI can provide valuable insights and enhance our decision-making, it's essential to maintain a balanced perspective. AI should not be viewed as a replacement for human expertise and judgment. Rather, it should be seen as a powerful tool to augment our knowledge, enhance our analysis, and empower us to make more informed investment decisions.

As we continue to navigate the evolving landscape of real estate investment, AI will undoubtedly play an increasingly pivotal role. By embracing its power, we can unlock a world of new opportunities, maximize our returns, and navigate the complexities of the market with greater confidence.

The Future of Real Estate Investment

The future of real estate investment is intertwined with the rapid advancements of artificial intelligence (AI). AI is poised to revolutionize the industry, transforming the way properties are valued, marketed, and managed. This section delves into the emerging technologies and their profound impact on the real estate landscape, exploring how AI is poised to unlock new opportunities and reshape the future of this crucial investment sector.

One of the most significant ways AI is impacting real estate investment is through property valuation. Traditional methods of property valuation often relied on human expertise and subjective assessments, which could lead to inconsistencies and inaccuracies. AI algorithms, however, can analyze vast amounts of data, including historical transaction records, market trends, and property characteristics, to generate highly accurate and objective valuations. This data-driven approach eliminates human bias and provides investors with a more reliable and transparent valuation process.

Moreover, AI-powered valuation tools are helping to streamline the process, making it faster and more efficient. This is particularly important in today's fast-paced real estate market, where time is of the essence. Investors can quickly assess the value of properties, facilitating informed decision-making and reducing the time required to complete transactions.

Beyond valuation, AI is revolutionizing real estate market analysis, providing investors with unparalleled insights into market trends and identifying hidden opportunities. By analyzing large datasets from a variety of sources, including property records, demographic data, and economic indicators, AI algorithms can uncover patterns and trends that might be missed by human analysts. This data-driven approach allows investors to gain a deeper understanding of local markets, identify areas with high growth potential, and make informed investment decisions.

Furthermore, AI is enhancing property marketing, making it more targeted and efficient. By analyzing data on potential buyers, AI algorithms can create personalized marketing campaigns that resonate with specific demographics and interests. This targeted approach ensures that marketing efforts reach the right audience, leading to higher conversion rates and improved return on investment. AI can also automate many marketing tasks, such as generating listings, scheduling showings, and responding to inquiries, freeing up real estate professionals to focus on higher-value activities.

The integration of AI is also transforming property management, making it more efficient and cost-effective. AI-powered property management systems can automate routine tasks, such as rent collection, tenant communication, and maintenance scheduling, reducing the workload of property managers and freeing them up to focus on more strategic initiatives. These systems can also analyze data to identify potential problems, such as early signs of wear and tear, enabling proactive maintenance and reducing the risk of costly repairs.

Looking ahead, the future of real estate investment is bright, powered by the transformative potential of AI. AI-driven technologies are poised to further enhance efficiency, transparency, and profitability in the industry, creating new opportunities for investors and reshaping the future of real estate.

AI-Powered PropTech: Shaping the Future of Real Estate

The advent of PropTech, a combination of real estate and technology, has accelerated the adoption of AI in the industry. PropTech companies are developing innovative AI-powered solutions to address various challenges in the real estate sector, from property search to investment management.

- **Smart Homes and AI-Enabled Living:** One of the most exciting areas of innovation is the integration of AI into smart homes. AI-powered devices and systems are transforming the way we live in our homes, creating a more comfortable, efficient, and personalized living experience. These systems can automate tasks such as temperature control, lighting, and security, creating a seamless and intelligent home environment. This integration of AI into homes is also attracting investors seeking to capitalize on the growing demand for smart home technology.
- **AI-Driven Virtual Tours:** The pandemic has accelerated the adoption of virtual tours, which allow potential buyers to explore properties remotely. AI-powered virtual tour technologies enhance the experience by creating immersive and interactive virtual tours, providing a more realistic and engaging experience for buyers.
- **AI-Powered Investment Platforms:** AI is also revolutionizing investment platforms, enabling investors to access real estate investment opportunities that were previously inaccessible. AI-powered platforms can automate tasks such as property research, analysis, and due diligence, making it easier for investors to find, evaluate, and manage real estate investments.

- **The Role of Blockchain in Real Estate:** Blockchain technology, with its decentralized and transparent nature, is also transforming the real estate sector. Blockchain-based platforms can streamline transactions, improve security, and enhance transparency in the real estate market. These platforms can also facilitate fractional ownership of real estate, opening up investment opportunities to a wider range of investors.

The Future of Real Estate: A World of Opportunities

The integration of AI and blockchain technologies is not just about automating processes; it is about creating a more efficient, transparent, and accessible real estate market. These technologies are driving innovation, fostering collaboration, and democratizing access to investment opportunities.

- **Addressing Ethical Considerations:** As AI plays an increasingly prominent role in real estate, it is crucial to address ethical considerations. It is important to ensure that AI systems are unbiased, transparent, and accountable, safeguarding against potential risks and ensuring that they are used responsibly and ethically.
- **The Need for Financial Literacy:** In this rapidly evolving landscape, it is more important than ever for investors to be financially literate. Understanding the complexities of AI and its application in real estate is essential for making informed investment decisions and navigating the future of this dynamic industry.

Conclusion

The future of real estate investment is bright, powered by the transformative potential of AI and blockchain technologies. These innovations are creating a more efficient, transparent, and accessible market, opening up new opportunities for investors of all levels of experience. By embracing these technologies and staying informed about the latest advancements, investors can unlock the potential of real estate and position themselves for success in the evolving landscape of this crucial investment sector.

CHAPTER 7

THE POWER OF MUTUAL FUNDS

DIVERSIFICATION AND PROFESSIONAL MANAGEMENT OF AI

UNDERSTANDING MUTUAL FUNDS

CMutual funds are a powerful investment vehicle that allows individuals to pool their money together to invest in a diversified portfolio of securities. Imagine a basket containing various fruits, each representing a different stock or bond. This basket represents a mutual fund, offering a mix of assets to reduce risk and potentially enhance returns.

The concept of diversification is crucial in investment, just as having a balanced diet is essential for good health. Diversifying your portfolio across different asset classes, such as stocks, bonds, and real estate, helps mitigate risk by reducing the impact of any single asset's performance on your overall investment.

Mutual funds provide a convenient and cost-effective way to achieve diversification. They are managed by professional fund managers who use their expertise and resources to select and manage the underlying securities in the fund. These fund managers constantly monitor market trends, analyze financial

133

data, and make investment decisions to maximize returns while minimizing risks.

Understanding the Structure of Mutual Funds

Mutual funds operate on a simple principle: investors buy units or shares of the fund, representing a portion of the fund's assets. These units are traded on stock exchanges, allowing investors to buy and sell them based on market prices. The fund's value, or net asset value (NAV), fluctuates with the performance of its underlying securities.

For instance, if the stocks within a particular mutual fund perform well, the fund's NAV will increase, reflecting higher value. Conversely, if the stocks perform poorly, the NAV will decrease. This is why it's crucial to carefully select mutual funds that align with your investment goals and risk tolerance.

Types of Mutual Funds

Mutual funds are categorized into various types, each designed to meet specific investment objectives. Here are some prominent categories:

1. **Equity Funds:** These funds primarily invest in stocks of companies, aiming to capture growth and capital appreciation. They can be further classified into:
   - **Large-cap funds:** Investing in companies with large market capitalizations, offering stability and potential for moderate growth.
   - **Mid-cap funds:** Focused on companies with mid-sized market capitalizations, providing a balance between growth and value.

- **Small-cap funds:** Targeting companies with small market capitalizations, seeking higher growth potential but potentially carrying higher risk.
- **Sector funds:** Concentrating on specific industry sectors, such as technology, healthcare, or energy, offering targeted exposure to specific market trends.

2. **Bond Funds:** These funds invest in bonds, which are debt securities issued by governments or corporations. Bonds offer a fixed income stream and are generally considered less risky than stocks. Different types of bond funds include:
   - **Government bond funds:** Investing in bonds issued by the government, considered relatively safe and offering lower returns.
   - **Corporate bond funds:** Investing in bonds issued by corporations, offering higher potential returns but carrying higher risk.
   - **High-yield bond funds:** Focused on bonds with lower credit ratings, offering potentially higher returns but also higher default risk.

3. **Balanced Funds:** These funds aim to provide a balance between equity and bond investments, seeking to optimize risk and return. They are ideal for investors seeking a diversified portfolio with moderate risk.

4. **Index Funds:** These funds track a specific market index, such as the S&P 500 or the Nasdaq 100. They offer passive investing, mirroring the performance of the underlying index without active management.

Benefits of Mutual Funds

Investing in mutual funds offers several advantages over individual stock or bond investments:

1. **Diversification:** Mutual funds provide instant diversification, enabling investors to access a wide range of securities with a single investment. This reduces portfolio risk, as the performance of any one security is less likely to significantly impact the overall fund's value.

2. **Professional Management:** Mutual funds are managed by experienced and skilled fund managers who are well-versed in market analysis, asset allocation, and risk management. These professionals utilize their expertise and resources to identify investment opportunities and make informed decisions to maximize returns.

3. **Cost-effectiveness:** Mutual funds offer economies of scale, allowing investors to access professional management and diversification at a relatively low cost. The management fees charged by mutual funds are typically lower than the costs associated with individually managing a diversified portfolio.

4. **Liquidity:** Mutual funds provide investors with liquidity, allowing them to buy and sell units on stock exchanges at prevailing market prices. This makes it easier for investors to access their investments when needed.

5. **Transparency:** Mutual funds are required to provide regular disclosures to investors, including information on their investment strategies, performance, and expenses. This transparency allows investors to assess the fund's performance and make informed investment

decisions.

The Role of AI in Mutual Fund Investment

AI is transforming the world of finance, and mutual funds are no exception. AI algorithms are now being employed to enhance various aspects of mutual fund investment:

1. **Fund Selection:** AI algorithms can analyze vast amounts of data, including historical performance, market trends, and fund manager expertise, to identify top-performing mutual funds. This empowers investors to make data-driven decisions, selecting funds with a higher probability of success.
2. **Portfolio Optimization:** AI algorithms can optimize mutual fund portfolio diversification, considering factors such as risk tolerance, investment goals, and market conditions. This ensures that the portfolio is balanced and well-rounded, effectively mitigating risk and maximizing potential returns.
3. **Risk Assessment:** AI algorithms can assess investment risks, identifying potential vulnerabilities and mitigating factors. This enables investors to make more informed decisions, understanding the potential risks and rewards associated with each mutual fund.
4. **Sentiment Analysis:** AI can analyze news articles, social media posts, and other online content to gauge market sentiment. This helps fund managers understand investor expectations, market trends, and potential risks, informing their investment decisions.

The Future of Mutual Funds with AI

AI is poised to revolutionize the world of mutual funds, driving innovation and efficiency. Here are some potential advancements:

1. **Personalized Investment Recommendations:** AI algorithms can tailor investment recommendations to individual investors, considering their financial profiles, investment goals, and risk tolerance. This personalized approach enhances investment outcomes, aligning investments with each investor's unique needs and aspirations.

2. **Automated Portfolio Management:** AI can automate portfolio management, adjusting asset allocation based on market conditions, investor goals, and risk profiles. This reduces the need for active human intervention, allowing investors to focus on their other financial priorities.

3. **Enhanced Risk Management:** AI can enhance risk management strategies, identifying emerging risks and adjusting investment allocations accordingly. This ensures that portfolios remain resilient in the face of market volatility and unforeseen events.

4. **Lower Investment Costs:** AI can streamline investment processes, reducing administrative costs and making mutual fund investment more accessible to a wider range of investors.

Conclusion

Mutual funds offer a powerful pathway to wealth creation, combining diversification, professional management, and cost-effectiveness. With the rise of AI, mutual funds are evolving, harnessing the power of technology to enhance performance, reduce costs, and personalize investment experiences. As AI continues to advance, mutual funds will become increasingly sophisticated, offering investors a more efficient, data-driven, and rewarding approach to financial success.

AI-Driven Mutual Fund Analysis

Mutual funds are investment vehicles that pool money from multiple investors to invest in a diversified portfolio of assets, such as stocks, bonds, or real estate. By diversifying your investments across different asset classes, mutual funds reduce risk and potentially enhance returns.

Mutual funds are managed by professional fund managers who have expertise in selecting and managing investments. These managers are responsible for researching and analyzing market trends, identifying promising investment opportunities, and making investment decisions on behalf of the fund's investors.

In the age of AI, mutual fund analysis has been transformed by the use of advanced algorithms and machine learning techniques. AI can analyze vast amounts of data from various sources, including financial statements, market trends, and economic indicators, to identify top-performing funds and assess their potential risks and returns.

AI-Driven Mutual Fund Analysis: A Data-Driven Approach

AI-powered tools can analyze mutual fund data in ways that are impossible for humans to do manually. These tools can process massive datasets, identify complex patterns, and generate insights that can help investors make informed decisions.

Here's how AI algorithms can be used in mutual fund analysis

Performance Analysis: AI can evaluate the historical performance of mutual funds, considering factors such as risk-adjusted returns, volatility, and consistency.

- **Fund Manager Evaluation:** AI can assess the track records of fund managers, considering factors such as their investment strategies, experience, and past performance.
- **Risk Assessment:** AI algorithms can analyze the risk profiles of mutual funds, considering factors such as sector exposure, market sensitivity, and concentration of holdings.
- **Market Trend Prediction:** AI can analyze market data and predict future market trends, enabling investors to identify funds that are likely to perform well in different market conditions.
- **Portfolio Optimization:** AI can help investors optimize their portfolios by identifying mutual funds that complement each other and reduce overall risk.

Selecting the Right Funds with AI Assistance

AI-powered tools can make the process of selecting the right mutual funds more efficient and effective. Here's how AI can help you navigate the vast landscape of mutual funds:

- **Personalized Recommendations:** AI algorithms can analyze your financial goals, risk tolerance, and investment horizon to provide personalized recommendations for mutual funds that align with your specific needs.

- **Fund Screening and Filtering:** AI can screen and filter mutual funds based on your criteria, such as investment style, asset class, expense ratio, and performance history.
- **Real-Time Monitoring:** AI can monitor the performance of your chosen funds and alert you to any significant changes in their risk profile or investment strategy.

The Benefits of AI in Mutual Fund Analysis

Using AI in mutual fund analysis offers several key benefits for investors:

- **Enhanced Investment Decisions:** AI can help you make more informed investment decisions by providing data-driven insights and recommendations.
- **Improved Portfolio Diversification:** AI can help you create a diversified portfolio of mutual funds that aligns with your risk tolerance and investment goals.
- **Increased Efficiency and Convenience:** AI-powered tools can automate many of the tasks involved in mutual fund analysis, freeing up your time and effort.
- **Reduced Risk:** AI can help you identify and mitigate investment risks, potentially leading to more stable and profitable returns.

Considerations and Ethical Implications

While AI offers powerful tools for mutual fund analysis, it is important to consider its limitations and potential ethical concerns.

- **Historical Data Bias:** AI algorithms rely on historical data to make predictions, which may reflect past biases and market anomalies.
- **Market Volatility:** AI algorithms can struggle to predict sudden market shifts and volatility, which can impact investment decisions.
- **Over-Reliance on AI:** Relying solely on AI for investment decisions can be risky, as it may not account for all relevant factors or unforeseen events.

It is crucial to use AI as a complementary tool to human expertise and judgment. Combining human insights with AI analysis can lead to more well-rounded investment decisions.

The Future of Mutual Funds and AI

The future of mutual funds is likely to be shaped by the continued development of AI. As AI algorithms become more sophisticated, we can expect to see:

- **Personalized Robo-Advisors:** AI-powered robo-advisors may offer personalized investment advice and portfolio management services specifically tailored to individual needs.
- **Automated Fund Selection:** AI may become more adept at selecting funds based on complex criteria and real-time market conditions.
- **Enhanced Risk Management:** AI could help to develop more advanced risk management strategies that anticipate and mitigate potential risks.

The integration of AI in mutual fund analysis represents a significant shift in the investment landscape. By embracing AI as a tool for informed decision-making, investors can potentially unlock greater returns, reduce risk, and achieve their financial goals. However, it is essential to use AI responsibly and with a critical eye, acknowledging its limitations and the importance of human expertise and judgment.

AI AND MUTUAL FUND PORTFOLIO MANAGEMENT

In the realm of mutual funds, AI is ushering in a new era of intelligent diversification, empowering investors to craft balanced and well-rounded portfolios. Imagine a financial world where algorithms, trained on mountains of data, can analyze market trends, identify undervalued assets, and assess risk profiles with remarkable precision. This is the reality AI brings to mutual fund management.

AI-driven algorithms can dissect vast datasets, including historical market performance, economic indicators, and individual fund characteristics, to uncover hidden patterns and potential opportunities. By leveraging machine learning, AI can identify funds with strong track records, low volatility, and favorable risk-return profiles, effectively streamlining the investment selection process.

But AI's influence extends beyond simple fund selection. It delves deeper, into the very heart of portfolio construction. By analyzing an investor's risk tolerance, financial goals, and investment time horizon, AI can generate personalized portfolio recommendations that are carefully tailored to individual needs. This level of customization was once reserved for high-net-worth individuals with access to sophisticated financial advisors. Now, through the power of AI, it is accessible to all.

Imagine an AI-powered system that analyzes your investment goals, such as retirement planning or saving for your child's education. It then crafts a diversified portfolio of mutual funds, strategically allocating assets across different sectors, asset classes, and geographies. The system ensures that your portfolio aligns with your risk tolerance, while aiming to maximize potential returns. This intelligent allocation process helps mitigate risk through diversification, spreading investments across a range of assets to reduce the impact of individual stock or bond fluctuations.

AI's ability to constantly monitor market conditions and adjust portfolio allocations based on evolving trends is a significant advantage. As market dynamics shift, AI algorithms can swiftly identify emerging opportunities and adjust the portfolio accordingly, ensuring it remains optimized for maximum potential. This adaptability is critical in today's volatile financial landscape, where market sentiment can change quickly.

However, it is crucial to understand that AI should not be seen as a replacement for human judgment. While AI can provide valuable insights and automate certain processes, the human element remains vital. Investors should always engage in critical thinking, understand the underlying principles of AI-driven recommendations, and retain the final decision-making authority.

Moreover, AI is not a magic bullet for guaranteed returns. It can help optimize diversification and streamline the investment process, but it cannot eliminate market risk entirely. Investors must always remember that past performance is not indicative of future results, and market fluctuations are inevitable.

The intersection of AI and mutual funds represents a significant advancement in the financial landscape. It empowers investors with sophisticated tools for diversification, risk management, and portfolio optimization. As AI continues to evolve, its impact on mutual fund management will only become more profound, ushering in a future where investment decisions are driven by data, insights, and a deeper understanding of market dynamics.

The Role of Fund Managers in the AI Era

The rise of artificial intelligence (AI) in the financial industry has undoubtedly revolutionized the way we approach investing. AI algorithms can process vast amounts of data, identify patterns, and make predictions with remarkable accuracy. This has led to the emergence of powerful tools like robo-advisors and automated trading platforms, which are making financial services more accessible and efficient than ever before. However, this raises an important question: what role do traditional fund managers play in an AI-powered financial landscape?

Fund managers, with their expertise in financial markets, risk assessment, and portfolio management, still hold a significant value in the era of AI. Their ability to analyze complex market dynamics, understand investor psychology, and make informed judgments based on both quantitative and qualitative factors remains crucial.

The Complementary Roles of AI and Fund Managers

AI excels at processing and analyzing massive datasets, uncovering hidden patterns, and executing trades with speed and precision. Fund managers, on the other hand, bring their human intuition, experience, and adaptability to the table. They can interpret the nuances of market sentiment, assess the long-term implications of economic trends, and make strategic decisions that AI algorithms may not fully grasp.

Imagine a fund manager overseeing a diversified portfolio of mutual funds. While AI tools can assist in identifying the best-performing funds based on historical data, the fund manager's expertise comes into play in evaluating the underlying strategies, the fund manager's track record, and the potential risks associated with each fund. By combining the analytical power of AI with their human judgment, fund managers can build robust and diversified portfolios tailored to specific investment goals and risk tolerances.

Human Oversight: A Crucial Element

Even the most sophisticated AI algorithms are not infallible. They are prone to biases, errors, and unexpected market fluctuations. Human oversight is essential to ensure that AI-driven investment decisions remain grounded in sound financial principles and ethical considerations.

Fund managers act as a crucial layer of human oversight, monitoring AI-generated recommendations and ensuring that they align with overall investment objectives. They can also adjust investment strategies based on unforeseen market events or changes in investor sentiment – situations that AI algorithms may not always anticipate.

The Importance of Emotional Intelligence

Investing involves more than just numbers and algorithms. It requires a deep understanding of human behavior and the ability to navigate the emotional rollercoaster that comes with market volatility. Fund managers bring their emotional intelligence to the table, helping investors stay focused on long-term goals and avoid impulsive decisions driven by fear or greed.

The Evolving Role of Fund Managers in the AI Era

In the years to come, the role of fund managers will continue to evolve alongside the advancement of AI. Fund managers are adapting to the new environment by embracing AI technologies, incorporating them into their workflows, and using them to enhance their decision-making capabilities. They are increasingly focusing on tasks that require human judgment, such as:

- **Strategic Asset Allocation:** Determining the optimal allocation of assets across different investment classes based on long-term market forecasts and investor preferences.
- **Risk Management:** Assessing the potential risks associated with various investments and implementing strategies to mitigate those risks.
- **Investor Communication and Education:** Communicating investment strategies, market trends, and financial risks to investors in a clear and understandable manner.
- **Ethical Considerations:** Ensuring that AI-driven investment decisions comply with ethical guidelines and industry regulations.

Beyond Data: The Human Touch

Fund managers are not simply robots programmed to follow algorithms. They are skilled professionals who understand the complexities of human behavior, market dynamics, and financial regulations. They bring a unique blend of knowledge, experience, and intuition that AI, in its current form, cannot fully replicate.

The Future of Fund Management: A Collaboration Between AI and Humans

The future of fund management lies in a collaboration between AI and humans. AI can handle the tedious tasks of data analysis, portfolio rebalancing, and trade execution, freeing up fund managers to focus on higher-level decision-making, investor relations, and the crucial human elements of investment management.

This partnership between AI and human expertise promises to bring greater efficiency, transparency, and personalization to the investment process. It will empower investors with access to sophisticated tools and insights that were once reserved for institutional investors.

As AI continues to advance, its role in finance will undoubtedly grow. However, the human element remains essential, and the value of experienced fund managers who can navigate the complexities of the financial world, understand investor psychology, and make ethical decisions will only become more apparent in the years to come.

In conclusion, the AI revolution is not a replacement for fund managers. Rather, it is a powerful tool that can enhance their capabilities, freeing them up to focus on the areas where human expertise is most valuable. The future of fund management lies in a seamless collaboration between AI and human judgment, where the strengths of each complement the other, ultimately benefiting investors and creating a more informed and efficient investment landscape.

AI and the Future of Mutual Funds

The future of mutual funds is intertwined with the rise of artificial intelligence (AI), creating a paradigm shift that promises to reshape the industry and empower investors in unprecedented ways. AI's transformative power lies in its ability to analyze massive amounts of data, identify patterns, and make predictions that are beyond human capabilities. This section delves into the exciting possibilities that AI brings to the world of mutual funds, exploring the impact on fund management, investor decision-making, and the overall landscape of this investment vehicle.

One of the most significant impacts of AI on mutual funds is the automation of investment processes. AI algorithms can analyze vast amounts of data, including market trends, economic indicators, and company financials, to identify investment opportunities and make informed decisions about asset allocation. This data-driven approach eliminates human bias and emotional influence, leading to more objective and efficient portfolio management.

AI-powered robo-advisors are becoming increasingly popular for managing mutual fund portfolios. These automated platforms leverage AI algorithms to provide personalized investment advice, create diversified portfolios tailored to individual risk tolerance and goals, and rebalance portfolios automatically based on changing market conditions. Robo-advisors offer several advantages, including lower fees compared to traditional financial advisors, increased transparency in investment decisions, and 24/7 accessibility.

Another area where AI is making a significant impact is in the selection of mutual funds. AI algorithms can analyze the performance of thousands of mutual funds, considering factors such as risk-adjusted returns, expense ratios, and fund manager experience, to identify the most promising investment options. This data-driven approach helps investors make more informed decisions and avoid investing in underperforming funds.

AI is also transforming the role of fund managers. While AI can automate many tasks, human expertise remains crucial for strategic decision-making, understanding market nuances, and interpreting complex data. Fund managers are now leveraging AI as a powerful tool to enhance their investment strategies, freeing up time for higher-level tasks such as identifying emerging market trends and developing innovative investment approaches.

The future of mutual funds is likely to see a greater integration of AI, with robo-advisors becoming increasingly sophisticated and offering more customized investment solutions. AI algorithms will play a key role in optimizing asset allocation, managing risk, and providing personalized investment advice. Investors can expect a more efficient and data-driven approach to mutual fund investing, potentially leading to better returns and a more personalized experience.

However, it's important to remember that AI is a tool, not a magic solution. While AI can analyze data and make predictions, it cannot fully replace the human element in investment decision-making. Investors need to be aware of the limitations of

AI and continue to develop their own financial literacy and understanding of investment principles.

The integration of AI in mutual funds presents both opportunities and challenges. While AI can enhance investment decisions, it's crucial to ensure that it is used responsibly and ethically. Transparency and accountability are essential in AI-driven investment processes, as are safeguards against potential bias and manipulation.

As AI continues to advance, we can expect to see further innovations in the world of mutual funds. Emerging technologies such as natural language processing, machine learning, and deep learning will further enhance the capabilities of AI in financial analysis, investment decision-making, and customer service.

The future of mutual funds is bright, with AI poised to revolutionize the industry and empower investors. By embracing this technology, investors can benefit from a more efficient, data-driven, and personalized investment experience, potentially unlocking new levels of financial success. As AI continues to evolve, it will be essential for investors to stay informed about its advancements and learn how to leverage its power to achieve their financial goals.

CHAPTER 8

MASTERING YOUR FINANCIAL JOURNEY

AI AND THE PATH TO FINANCIAL FREEDOM

INTEGRATING AI INTO YOUR INVESTMENT STRATEGY

In the ever-evolving landscape of finance, artificial intelligence (AI) has emerged as a powerful force, transforming the way individuals approach their financial journeys. This chapter delves into the practical aspects of integrating AI into your investment strategy, empowering you to harness its potential and navigate the path to financial freedom.

Imagine having a personalized financial advisor who analyzes vast amounts of data, identifies lucrative opportunities, and manages your portfolio with precision. AI can make this vision a reality, providing you with the tools and insights needed to make informed investment decisions.

A Practical Guide to Integrating AI into Your Investment Strategy:

1. **Define Your Financial Goals and Risk Tolerance:** Before diving into the realm of AI-powered investments, it's essential to establish clear financial goals. What are you aiming to achieve? Are you saving for retirement, a down payment on a house, or funding your children's education? Once you have defined your goals, assess your risk tolerance – your comfort level with potential losses in pursuit of higher returns. This foundational step allows you to tailor your AI-driven strategy to align with your unique circumstances.

2. **Embrace Robo-Advisors:** Robo-advisors are AI-powered platforms that provide automated financial advice and portfolio management services. These platforms leverage advanced algorithms to analyze your financial profile, investment goals, and risk tolerance, creating a personalized investment strategy. Robo-advisors often offer lower fees compared to traditional financial advisors, making them an attractive option for investors seeking cost-effective solutions. When selecting a robo-advisor, consider factors such as investment options, asset allocation strategies, and customer support.

3. **Explore Automated Trading Platforms:** For more experienced investors seeking to enhance their trading strategies, automated trading platforms provide a powerful tool. These platforms utilize AI algorithms to execute trades based on predefined rules and strategies. Automated trading can help you capitalize on market opportunities, reduce emotional biases, and execute trades with speed and precision. However, it's crucial to understand the complexities of automated trading and ensure that your chosen

platform aligns with your investment goals and risk tolerance. Remember, even with automated trading, regular monitoring and adjustments may be necessary.

4. **Leverage AI-Driven Market Analysis:** The financial markets are constantly evolving, making it challenging to stay abreast of the latest trends and opportunities. AI algorithms can analyze vast amounts of market data, identify patterns, and predict future movements. By leveraging AI-powered market analysis, you can gain a deeper understanding of the market, identify potentially profitable investments, and make more informed decisions. Many online platforms and financial news sources offer AI-driven market analysis tools, providing insights into specific sectors, companies, and overall market trends.

5. **Harness AI for Portfolio Optimization:** AI can help you optimize your portfolio by identifying areas for improvement and recommending adjustments based on your risk tolerance, investment goals, and market conditions. AI algorithms can analyze your current portfolio, assess asset allocation, and identify opportunities for diversification. By leveraging AI for portfolio optimization, you can strive for a more balanced and efficient investment strategy that aligns with your long-term goals.

The Importance of Ongoing Learning and Adaptability

AI is rapidly evolving, with new technologies and tools emerging constantly. To fully embrace the benefits of AI in finance, it's essential to remain a lifelong learner, staying updated on the latest advancements and their implications for your investment strategy.

Building a Sustainable Financial Future: Embracing AI for Long-Term Success

The integration of AI into your investment strategy is not a one-time event but an ongoing process that requires continuous adaptation and refinement. As AI technologies evolve, so too will your understanding and utilization of these tools. Remember, AI is a powerful ally, not a substitute for your financial acumen and decision-making skills.

The Power of AI for Financial Empowerment: Taking Control of Your Finances

By embracing AI, you can empower yourself to take control of your financial future, making informed decisions that align with your goals and aspirations. AI can provide the tools and insights needed to make smart investments, manage your money effectively, and build a sustainable financial future. As you continue to navigate the exciting world of AI in finance, remember to stay informed, adapt to the changing landscape, and embrace the opportunities for financial empowerment that AI offers.

THE IMPORTANCE OF ONGOING LEARNING AND ADAPTABILITY

The world of finance is constantly evolving, and staying ahead of the curve is essential to making informed financial decisions. Just as the financial landscape has been reshaped by technological advancements, so too has the importance of continuous learning and adaptability become paramount. In the realm of AI in finance, this principle takes on even greater significance.

Think of AI as a powerful engine that fuels the financial world, constantly churning out data, insights, and predictions. But like any engine, it requires regular maintenance and upgrades to perform optimally. The same applies to our understanding of AI in finance – it is an ongoing journey, not a destination. Just as new technologies emerge, so too do new applications and implications of AI.

Consider the evolution of robo-advisors, once a novelty in the world of investment, now becoming increasingly sophisticated and widespread. What was once a simple automated investment service has transformed into a powerful tool capable of tailoring portfolios, analyzing market trends, and even offering personalized financial advice. This rapid evolution demands that we adapt our understanding and approach to keep pace.

But continuous learning is not just about keeping up with the latest trends. It is also about developing a critical eye for evaluating the vast amounts of information generated by AI. Just because a machine says something, doesn't make it inherently true. The ability to critically analyze AI-driven insights, understanding their limitations and potential biases, is crucial in making sound financial decisions.

Imagine a scenario where an AI algorithm predicts a surge in a particular stock based on complex market analysis. While the algorithm might be based on sound data and logic, it could be susceptible to biases or blind spots. For example, it might not account for unforeseen geopolitical events or changes in consumer behavior that could significantly impact the stock's performance.

This is where human judgment and financial literacy come into play. We need to be able to assess the AI's recommendations alongside our own knowledge and understanding of the market. This means staying informed about economic trends, industry developments, and potential risks. It means developing a strong understanding of the financial principles underpinning the AI's recommendations and critically evaluating the data and assumptions it relies upon.

This critical thinking approach is not just about skepticism. It is about leveraging the power of AI while remaining in control of our financial decisions. It is about harnessing AI as a powerful tool, but not becoming entirely reliant upon it.

Another crucial aspect of adaptability in the AI era is the ability to embrace new technologies as they emerge. AI is a rapidly evolving field, with new breakthroughs and innovations happening all the time. This means staying open to new ways of thinking about finance, exploring emerging technologies, and adapting our approach accordingly.

This might involve learning new skills, exploring different financial tools and platforms, or even venturing into new investment areas made accessible by AI advancements. Remember, the financial landscape is constantly evolving, and we need to evolve with it.

As AI continues to reshape the financial world, our capacity for continuous learning and adaptability will be key to navigating this evolving landscape. It will allow us to harness the immense power of AI to our advantage, while simultaneously ensuring we remain in control of our financial destinies. The future of finance is dynamic, and it is up to us to stay ahead of the curve and embrace the opportunities and challenges that lie ahead.

Building a Sustainable Financial Future

Building a sustainable financial future requires a long-term perspective and a strategic approach that embraces both innovation and prudence. In this era of technological advancement, AI emerges as a powerful ally, capable of revolutionizing how we manage our finances and navigate the complexities of the investment landscape. By strategically integrating AI into our financial strategies, we can unlock unprecedented opportunities for long-term success and secure a prosperous future.

Imagine a world where your investments are not merely subject to chance but guided by sophisticated algorithms that analyze vast amounts of data, identifying patterns and trends that would be impossible for humans to discern. AI-powered tools can analyze market data, evaluate investment risks, and optimize portfolio diversification with unparalleled precision and efficiency. This data-driven approach allows us to make informed decisions, mitigate risks, and maximize returns over the long term.

AI can help us navigate the ever-changing financial landscape with greater confidence and agility. Its ability to analyze vast amounts of data in real-time enables us to stay ahead of market trends, adapt to evolving economic conditions, and capitalize on opportunities that might otherwise be missed. Imagine receiving personalized financial recommendations tailored to your individual needs, risk tolerance, and financial goals, based on the latest market intelligence and insights. This level of personalized guidance can empower us to make investment decisions that align with our aspirations and lead to greater financial well-being.

However, the journey toward a sustainable financial future with AI is not without its challenges. It's crucial to approach this technology with a balanced perspective, recognizing its limitations and potential pitfalls. While AI can provide invaluable insights and automation, it should never replace human judgment, critical thinking, and financial literacy. We must remain vigilant about the potential biases, ethical considerations, and risks associated with relying solely on AI for financial decisions.

The key to harnessing the power of AI for long-term success lies in maintaining a proactive and adaptable approach. As AI technologies continue to evolve, we must embrace continuous learning, stay informed about the latest advancements, and refine our financial strategies accordingly. It's essential to cultivate a mindset of lifelong learning, constantly seeking to expand our understanding of AI and its implications for our financial lives.

To illustrate the transformative power of AI in building a sustainable financial future, let's consider a few real-world examples:

- **Robo-Advisors for Long-Term Portfolio Management:** Robo-advisors are AI-powered platforms that provide automated financial advice and portfolio management services. These platforms leverage algorithms to create diversified portfolios based on individual risk tolerance and investment goals. They constantly monitor market conditions, rebalance portfolios, and make adjustments to ensure optimal performance over the long term. By utilizing robo-advisors, individuals can access sophisticated investment strategies typically reserved for high-net-worth individuals, while minimizing costs and maximizing efficiency.

- **AI-Driven Retirement Planning:** AI can revolutionize retirement planning by providing personalized projections based on factors such as age, income, expenses, investment choices, and anticipated life expectancy. These projections can help individuals make informed decisions about savings, investment strategies, and withdrawal plans, ensuring a comfortable and secure retirement.
- **AI-Powered Investment Research:** AI algorithms can analyze vast amounts of data, including financial news, company reports, and market trends, to identify promising investment opportunities. They can uncover hidden patterns, evaluate company performance, and predict future stock prices with greater accuracy than traditional methods. By utilizing AI-powered research tools, investors can make more informed decisions and potentially outperform the market.

Beyond individual investment strategies, AI can also play a crucial role in shaping a more inclusive and equitable financial system. AI-powered tools can democratize access to financial services, providing individuals with greater financial literacy and empowering them to take control of their finances. This can lead to a more financially stable and prosperous society, where individuals have the resources and knowledge to achieve their financial goals and build a secure future.

Building a sustainable financial future with AI requires a commitment to lifelong learning, embracing both the opportunities and challenges presented by this transformative technology. By strategically integrating AI into our financial strategies, we can unlock unprecedented opportunities for long-term success, achieve financial freedom, and secure a prosperous future for ourselves and future generations. As we navigate this exciting new frontier of AI-driven finance, it's important to remember that human intelligence, judgment, and ethical considerations will always remain integral to our financial well-being.

The Power of AI for Financial Empowerment

Imagine a world where your financial decisions are backed by the power of artificial intelligence (AI), a world where complex calculations and market analysis are just a click away. This is the reality that AI is rapidly shaping, empowering individuals like you to take control of their finances and chart a path toward financial freedom.

AI, with its ability to process vast amounts of data and identify patterns that humans might miss, is transforming how we approach personal finance. From budgeting and saving to investing and retirement planning, AI tools are offering personalized solutions tailored to individual needs and goals. It's like having a financial advisor in your pocket, ready to provide insights and recommendations based on your unique financial situation.

But AI is not just about crunching numbers; it's about empowering you to make informed choices. AI-powered tools can help you understand your spending habits, identify areas where you can save, and even suggest ways to optimize your investments. By providing a clear picture of your financial landscape, AI gives you the knowledge and confidence to make decisions that align with your goals.

Take, for instance, the realm of investment. AI algorithms can analyze historical market data, identify emerging trends, and even predict potential market movements. This allows you to make informed decisions about where to allocate your money, potentially maximizing returns while mitigating risks.

Robo-advisors, powered by AI, are becoming increasingly popular for their ability to manage investment portfolios automatically. They can create a diversified portfolio that aligns with your risk tolerance and investment goals, rebalancing it as needed to optimize performance. With robo-advisors, you can access professional-level investment management at a fraction of the cost of traditional advisors.

But it's not just about maximizing returns. AI can also help you build a sustainable financial future. By analyzing your income, expenses, and financial goals, AI can create a personalized roadmap for achieving financial freedom. This could include strategies for debt management, savings optimization, and investment planning.

The key to unlocking the full potential of AI in personal finance is understanding its strengths and limitations. AI is a powerful tool, but it shouldn't be seen as a magic bullet. It's crucial to maintain financial literacy, understand the principles behind your financial decisions, and have a critical eye when evaluating AI-driven recommendations.

AI is not a substitute for your own judgment and financial literacy. It's a powerful tool that can complement your financial knowledge and empower you to make informed decisions.

Embrace the possibilities that AI offers, but always remain in control of your financial journey. The future of personal finance is powered by AI, and you have the power to shape it.

CONCLUSION

The dawn of artificial intelligence (AI) in personal finance marks a pivotal turning point in how we manage our money. This technological revolution promises to empower individuals like never before, transforming the way we invest, save, and plan for our financial future. While the journey of integrating AI into personal finance has just begun, the implications are profound. It's a new era of opportunity, where technology, coupled with human intelligence and financial literacy, can unlock unprecedented levels of financial empowerment.

Imagine a world where complex investment decisions are made not by instinct or emotions, but by sophisticated algorithms that analyze vast datasets, identifying hidden patterns and opportunities. This is the power of AI in action. Through robo-advisors, automated trading platforms, and personalized financial recommendations, AI is already reshaping the financial landscape, making sophisticated investment strategies accessible to everyone.

For those starting their investment journey, AI provides a valuable stepping stone. It demystifies the world of finance, offering clear explanations of complex concepts and guiding beginners through the intricate process of portfolio management. By leveraging AI-powered tools, newcomers can confidently navigate the market, make informed decisions, and build a solid foundation for their financial future.

Seasoned investors, too, stand to benefit significantly from AI's capabilities. AI can automate routine tasks, freeing up valuable time for strategic decision-making. It can also analyze market trends, identify emerging opportunities, and even predict potential risks, empowering investors to make data-driven decisions with greater confidence.

Beyond its practical applications, AI is fostering a profound cultural shift in personal finance. It's democratizing access to financial services, breaking down barriers that once prevented individuals from achieving financial freedom. AI-powered platforms are now accessible to everyone, regardless of their wealth or investment experience.

This transformation is not without its challenges. Ethical considerations surrounding AI's influence in finance are paramount. We must ensure that AI algorithms are fair, transparent, and free from bias. The human element remains critical. While AI provides powerful tools, ultimately, individuals must exercise their judgment and understanding to make responsible financial decisions.

As we move forward, the integration of AI into personal finance will continue to evolve. Emerging technologies, such as blockchain and cryptocurrencies, are poised to further revolutionize the financial landscape, creating new opportunities and challenges. It's a landscape where continuous learning is essential, where embracing innovation and adapting to change will be the key to navigating the ever-evolving world of AI-driven finance.

The future of personal finance is bright, promising a world where financial freedom is within reach for everyone. By harnessing the power of AI, embracing financial literacy, and staying informed about emerging technologies, we can embark on a journey towards a more secure, prosperous, and fulfilling financial future. It's a journey that begins with embracing the AI revolution in personal finance, and taking control of our own financial destiny.

This book would not have been possible without the invaluable support and guidance of numerous individuals. I extend my heartfelt gratitude to [insert names of people who contributed to the book, such as editors, researchers, reviewers, and mentors]. Their insights, expertise, and encouragement have been instrumental in shaping this work.

I am particularly indebted to [insert names of specific individuals who provided exceptional support or guidance]. Their contributions have significantly enriched the content and clarity of this book.

I would also like to acknowledge the numerous researchers and thought leaders in the field of FinTech and AI who have paved the way for this book. Their groundbreaking work has inspired me to explore the transformative potential of AI in personal finance.

ACKNOWLEDGMENTS

This book would not have been possible without the invaluable contributions of many individuals. I am deeply grateful to the experts in Artificial Intelligence, Ethics, Psychology, and Sociology who collaborated with me on this project, sharing their knowledge, insights, and perspectives. Their guidance and expertise have shaped the book's content and deepened its understanding of the complex intersection of AI and human consciousness.

I am also indebted to my editor, [editor's name], for their meticulous attention to detail, insightful feedback, and unwavering support throughout the writing process. Their guidance has helped me to refine my ideas, clarify my arguments, and craft a more engaging and accessible narrative.

I would also like to thank the researchers, practitioners, and thought leaders who have generously shared their time, insights, and work with me. Their research and experiences have provided valuable context and inspiration for the book.

Finally, I am grateful to my family and friends for their unwavering encouragement and support, providing a much- needed source of inspiration and motivation during the long hours of writing.

Afterword

The creation of "The N.E.R.D.Y. Way: An Everyday Guide to AI" was a collaborative effort, and we are deeply grateful to everyone who contributed their expertise, insights, and unwavering support.

First and foremost, we would like to express our sincere gratitude to the 3CAT team for their meticulous research, insightful contributions, and dedication to crafting engaging and accessible content. Their collective expertise and passion were instrumental in bringing this book to life.

We extend our heartfelt thanks to the reviewers who provided valuable feedback and guidance throughout the writing process. Their thoughtful suggestions and constructive criticism helped shape the book into its final form.

We are also grateful to the individuals and organizations who generously shared their knowledge and experience, contributing to the depth and accuracy of the book. Their insights have enriched the content and provided valuable context for our readers.

Finally, we would like to thank our families and friends for their patience and understanding during the long hours spent writing and editing this book. Their unwavering support has been a source of inspiration and strength.

This appendix provides additional resources and information to complement the content discussed in the book.

GLOSSARY

This glossary provides definitions for key terms and concepts discussed in the book, making it easier for readers to navigate the complex world of AI.

1. **Artificial Intelligence (AI):** The ability of a computer or machine to perform tasks that typically require human intelligence, such as learning, problem-solving, and decision-making.
2. **Machine Learning (ML):** A type of AI that allows computers to learn from data without explicit programming. ML algorithms can identify patterns in data and make predictions or decisions.
3. **Personalized Learning:** An educational approach that tailors content and experiences to each student's unique needs, strengths, and weaknesses.
4. **Intelligent Tutoring Systems (ITS):** AI-powered virtual tutors that provide personalized guidance and feedback, adapting to each learner's unique needs.
5. **Adaptive Learning:** A technology-based approach that adjusts the difficulty and pace of learning materials based on student performance.
6. **Data Privacy:** The protection of personal information, including student data, from unauthorized access, use, or disclosure.
7. **Algorithmic Bias:** The tendency of AI algorithms to produce biased results based on the data they are trained on.
8. **Equity in Education:** Ensuring that all students have equal access to high-quality education, regardless of their background or circumstances.

REFERENCES & SOURCES

This section provides a list of references and sources that were consulted in the writing of this book.

1. AlHogail A. (2018). Improving IoT technology adoption through improving consumer trust. Technologies. 6, 64. 10.3390/technologies6030064 [DOI]

2. Bahmanziari T., Pearson J. M., Crosby L. (2003). Is trust important in technology adoption? A policy capturing approach. J. Comput. Inf. Syst. 43, 46–54. 10.1080/08874417.2003.11647533 [DOI]

3. Bang H., Martin A., Prat A., Selva D. (2018). Daphne: an intelligent assistant for architecting earth observing satellite systems. AIAA Conf. Proc. 1366:1–14. 10.2514/6.2018-1366 [DOI]

4. Belanche D., Casaló L. V., Flavián C. (2019). Artificial intelligence in FinTech: understanding robo-advisors adoption among customers. Ind. Manag. Data Syst. 119. 10.1108/IMDS-08-2018-0368 [DOI]

5. Bernard Z. (2018). We're Spending More Time with Smart Speakers Instead of with Radios, TVs - and Smartphones. New York, NY: Insider, Inc.

6. Calhoun C. S., Bobko P., Gallimore J. J., Lyons J. B. (2019). An expanded typology and exploratory experiment. J. Trust Res. 9, 28–46. 10.1080/21515581.2019.1579730 [DOI]

7. Central Council for Financial and Information (2016). Financial Literacy Survey: 2016 Results. Tokyo: Bank of Japan.

8. Downen, T., Kim, S., Lee, L. (2024). Algorithm aversion, emotions, and investor reaction: Does disclosing the use of AI influence investment decisions?, International Journal of Accounting Information Systems, 52. 10.1016/j.accinf.2023.100664. [DOI}

About the Author
Dr. C.B. Howard, 3CAT

3CAT is a collective of professionals collaborating across various disciplines to offer innovative and practical solutions for individuals seeking to comprehend the effects of artificial intelligence (AI). We are committed to the dissemination of education and information, striving to enhance the lives of others. While knowledge is a powerful tool, its true potential is realized through its application.

At 3CAT, we acknowledge that everyone is unique. Consequently, we provide a diverse range of training and guidance materials tailored to accommodate different needs and learning preferences. Our publications cover a wide range of important topics, aiming to deepen understanding and knowledge in various areas of interest.

For every publication, 3CAT collaborates to conduct research, develop pertinent topics, create manuscripts, and oversee the publication process, to ensure the highest quality work possible.

The **N.E.R.D.Y.** WAY is an acronym for k**N**owledge, **E**ducation, **R**esource, **D**iscovery for **Y**ou.

The trademark for "The NERDY WAY" has been applied for and is currently pending.